Lecture Notes in Computer Science 14095

Founding Editors

Gerhard Goos
Juris Hartmanis

W0079937

The series Lecture Notes in Computer Science (LNCS), including its subseries Lecture Notes in Artificial Intelligence (LNAI) and Lecture Notes in Bioinformatics (LNBI), has established itself as a medium for the publication of new developments in computer science and information technology research, teaching, and education.

LNCS enjoys close cooperation with the computer science R & D community, the series counts many renowned academics among its volume editors and paper authors, and collaborates with prestigious societies. Its mission is to serve this international community by providing an invaluable service, mainly focused on the publication of conference and workshop proceedings and postproceedings. LNCS commenced publication in 1973.

Andrew Reynolds · Serdar Tasiran

Editors

Verified Software

Theories, Tools and Experiments

15th International Conference, VSTTE 2023
Ames, IA, USA, October 23–24, 2023
Revised Selected Papers

 Springer

Editors
Andrew Reynolds
University of Iowa
Iowa City, IA, USA

Serdar Tasiran
Amazon Web Services
New York, NY, USA

ISSN 0302-9743   ISSN 1611-3349 (electronic)
Lecture Notes in Computer Science
ISBN 978-3-031-66063-4   ISBN 978-3-031-66064-1 (eBook)
https://doi.org/10.1007/978-3-031-66064-1

This Springer imprint is published by the registered company Springer Nature Switzerland AG
The registered company address is: Gewerbestrasse 11, 6330 Cham, Switzerland

If disposing of this product, please recycle the paper.

Preface

This volume contains the papers presented at VSTTE 2023: International Conference on Verified Software: Theories, Tools, and Experiments, held on October 23, 2023 in Ames, Iowa. It was co-located with Formal Methods in Computer-Aided Design 2023.

The program included 6 papers chosen out of 13 submissions using double-blind reviews. Each submission was reviewed by 3 program committee members. The program also included two invited talks and two invited tutorials. Peter Müller (ETH Zurich) gave an invited talk titled "Verified Secure Routing" and Arie Gurfinkel (University of Waterloo) gave an invited talk titled "Verifying Verified Code". The two invited tutorials were both by scientists from Amazon Web Services. Robert Jones gave a tutorial titled "Solving in the Cloud, for the Cloud" and Mike Hicks gave a tutorial titled "Cedar: A language for expressing fast, safe, and fine-grained authorization policies".

The goal of the VSTTE conference series is to advance the state of the art in the science and technology of software verification, through the interaction of theory development, tool evolution, and experimental validation.

The Verified Software Initiative (VSI), spearheaded by Tony Hoare and Jayadev Misra, is a research program for making large-scale verified software a practical reality. The International Conference on Verified Software: Theories, Tools, and Experiments (VSTTE) is the main forum for advancing the initiative. VSTTE brings together experts spanning the spectrum of software verification in order to foster international collaboration on the critical research challenges. The theoretical work includes semantic foundations and logics for specification and verification, and verification algorithms and methodologies. The tools cover specification and annotation languages, program analyzers, model checkers, interactive verifiers and proof checkers, automated theorem provers and SAT/SMT solvers, and integrated verification environments. The experimental work drives the research agenda for theory and tools by taking on significant specification/verification exercises covering hardware, operating systems, compilers, computer security, parallel computing, and cyber-physical systems.

May 2024

Serdar Tasiran
Andrew Reynolds

Organization

Program Committee

Christel Baier	TU Dresden, Germany
Haniel Barbosa	Universidade Federal de Minas Gerais, Brazil
Roderick Bloem	TU Graz, Austria
Borzoo Bonakdarpour	Michigan State University, USA
Supratik Chakraborty	IIT Bombay, India
Constantin Enea	École Polytechnique, France
Grigory Fedyukovich	Florida State University, USA
Pierre-Loic Garoche	ENAC, France
Ahmed Irfan	SRI International, USA
Burcu Kulahcioglu Ozkan	Delft University of Technology, Netherlands
Akash Lal	Microsoft, India
Sergio Mover	École Polytechnique, France
Carlos Olarte	LIPN, Université Sorbonne Paris Nord, France
Gennaro Parlato	University of Molise, Italy
Andrew Reynolds (Chair)	University of Iowa, USA
Kristin Yvonne Rozier	Iowa State University, USA
Serdar Tasiran (Chair)	Amazon, USA
Stefano Tonetta	FBK, Italy
Hiroshi Unno	University of Tsukuba, Japan
Yakir Vizel	Technion, Israel
Yuepeng Wang	Simon Fraser University, Canada
Kirsten Winter	University of Queensland, Australia
Pamela Zave	Princeton University, USA

Contents

Contents

Picky CDCL: SMT-Solving with Flexible Literal Selection

Konstantin I. Britikov[1]([⊠]), Antti E. J. Hyvärinen[2]([⊠]),
and Natasha Sharygina[1]([⊠])

[1] USI, Lugano, Switzerland
{britik,sharygin}@usi.ch
[2] Certora, Lugano, Switzerland
antti@certora.com

Abstract. SMT solvers have traditionally been optimized for determining the satisfiability of a query as quickly as possible. However, they are increasingly being used in applications where the time required to determine satisfiability might not be the main concern, such as mining inductive invariants for safety proofs.

This paper studies how lookahead-inspired SMT solving, when made sufficiently efficient and integrated into a conflict-driven, clause learning SMT core, can be a valuable component in a portfolio for proof-based interpolation in model checking.

We implemented the algorithmic idea, called Picky CDCL, in the SMT solver OpenSMT and show its efficiency in the Horn solver Golem using a range of model checking approaches and in SMT proof validation applications.

Keywords: Lookahead · CDCL · SMT · CHC · Formal Verification · DRAT Proofs · Interpolants

1 Introduction

The success of modern tools for determining satisfiability of propositional and first-order logic instances using SAT and SMT solving is often interpreted as resulting from how they combine the search for a satisfiable assignment with the search of a refutation for satisfiability [29]. This idea carries over to model checking, where many tools combine a search for a safe, inductive invariant with the search for a counter-example to correctness [6,18,21,23]. This works particularly well when proof-based Craig interpolation is integrated into the process [1,10,24]. Making this type of model checking efficient requires tight integration with one or more SAT or SMT solvers. As a result, the highly tuned setup might suffer from a lack of diversity in the solving approaches, meaning that corner cases, typically proofs, can be very hard to prove or the model checker might deviate instead of finding the proof.

This paper addresses this problem by studying a modification for the SMT-based search for models and refutations that is sufficiently efficient to solve existing benchmarks, but at the same time different from the standard approaches to provide a somewhat orthogonal search.

© The Author(s), under exclusive license to Springer Nature Switzerland AG 2024
A. Reynolds and S. Tasiran (Eds.): VSTTE 2023, LNCS 14095, pp. 1–19, 2024.
https://doi.org/10.1007/978-3-031-66064-1_1

The idea is a new Conflict Driven Clause Learning (CDCL) - based procedure with flexible breadth-first literal selection, which we call Picky CDCL. Our algorithm combines the lookahead [17] style search and Variable State Independent Decaying Sum (VSIDS) [26] SAT heuristics. To pick a literal for propagation, the lookahead algorithm first evaluates all of the undefined literals one by one. It calculates the impact of each literal propagation by determining the number of automatic subsequent propagations it would trigger (due to the clauses with a single undefined literal remaining, so-called unit clauses). Once it has evaluated all of the literals, it selects the one with the highest impact and performs the actual propagation. While it naturally results in a slower solving process (as compared to the VSIDS approach) it guarantees a more careful pick of the literal. VSIDS on the other hand keeps count of the literal usage in the instance and picks the literal that occurs most frequently in the conflicts.

Picky CDCL aims to strike a balance between the speed of the VSIDS algorithm and the careful literal selection of the lookahead search. Rather than relying solely on literal scoring provided by VSIDS, during each propagation, Picky CDCL selects ω literals with the best VSIDS scores and subsequently performs a lookahead procedure for these selected literals. The use of CDCL and consideration of multiple literals at each stage results in a more detailed decision tree and additional clauses that consequently might result in the artifacts better suitable for verification purposes (for example, better quality interpolants generated by the interpolating SMT solvers). This paper explores the impact of this potentially slower but more careful approach on the production of DRAT proofs and interpolants. We implemented our algorithm in the OpenSMT solver [20] and discovered that the Constrained Horn Clauses (CHC) solver using OpenSMT enhanced with Picky CDCL was able to solve a set of CHC instances that could not be solved by a competitive CHC solver with the use of the classical VSIDS-based algorithm, and demonstrated uniqueness using the random seed testing. We discovered that the portfolio, which includes VSIDS and Picky-CDCL, is significantly more performant than pure VSIDS or Picky-CDCL approaches. Additionally, our experimentation revealed that the SMT solver with Picky CDCL was able to significantly decrease the proof validation time.

Overall, the contributions of this paper are the definition and implementation of the Picky CDCL algorithm. It can act as a CDCL(T)-VSIDS hybrid extension, a classical lookahead, and more importantly as a mixed approach all of which can be defined by the configuration of the algorithm. This allows one to optimize the selection of literals while maintaining the efficiency of the search. While the mixed approach is more flexible in its search, it naturally benefits from the performance efficiency of the classical algorithms. When the mixed approach is used in the SMT-based verification, due to the increased amount of literal propagations, it results in slower performance as compared to classical VSIDS. Our experimentation demonstrates that this overhead is not substantial. Nonetheless, as confirmed by our extensive evaluation, it allows for the potential discovery of shorter and more precise solutions better suitable for the verification tasks.

The rest of the paper is structured as follows: Next subsection provides background in the related work. The section on preliminaries provides a brief overview of the relevant concepts and technologies. The main contribution of the paper, Picky CDCL algorithm with flexible literal selection, is presented in detail in Sect. 3. In Sect. 4, the effectiveness of the approach is evaluated through a series of experiments, including its application in CHC solving and DRAT proofs production, as well as an analysis of its overhead. The paper concludes with a summary of the main findings and suggestions for future work in Sect. 5.

Related Work

This work builds upon the CDCL [29,31] and DPLL [4,11] approaches for SAT solving, which were later adapted for use in SMT. The CDCL algorithm is a conflict-driven methodology that operates by backtracking when conflicts are encountered and utilizing the resulting information to generate clauses that restrict the assignment of literals causing the conflicts.

Our technique is significantly influenced by the Variable State Independent Decaying Sum (VSIDS) heuristics [26], which greatly improves the splitting part of DPLL(T) by quickly selecting literals for splitting based on their frequency of occurrence in clauses. VSIDS is a widely used heuristic in many solvers, resulting in minimal time spent on selecting literals for branching.

The development and application of the lookahead heuristics in SAT and SMT solving have a key importance for our work. The core idea of a lookahead SAT solver is to propagate all literals and select the one that leads to the most collateral propagations, repeating the process until all literals are propagated [8]. The first lookahead-based solver [8] was developed in 1996 and was a top-performing SAT solver at the time. Lookahead has since been adopted by several major SAT/SMT solvers, such as Z3 [15,27], where it is used for selecting cubes for splitting in the SAT solver core [15]. Recently, the lookahead algorithm was applied to SMT solving in the OpenSMT solver. This implementation showed improvements over VSIDS on certain benchmark sets, even though it used a significant amount of additional propagations, checking all literals at each step, even previously checked ones. This approach was particularly designed for constructing evenly-sized subproblems to partition a search space in parallel solving. We differ in the current work from [20] in that we overcome the performance bottleneck and do not maintain a DPLL-style tree for the parallelization.

The closest topic to this work is a combination and refitting of SAT/SMT heuristics. Mixing of lookahead and VSIDS in SAT solving applications was mentioned in the [33] as a means to break equality between the VSIDS scores to increase the performance of a solver. If the scores are the same, lookahead is used on the literals with equivalent scores to pick the literal for propagation. Unfortunately, this approach did not lead to a speedup in the solving process. Unlike the aforementioned approach, we used a limited version of the lookahead which runs at each decision level during the solving process. Lookahead is executed on a certain amount of top-scored VSIDS literals, not necessarily with the same score. Our goal in this work was to increase the amount of information we get during solving, while remaining performant in terms of deciding satisfiability. The ultimate goal of our solution is not to improve the performance of the solver but to produce a solution that contains more information suitable for verification tasks. In our experimentation with several verification tools, we observed that Picky CDCL achieves this goal.

In recent years, significant efforts have been made in the production of proofs (see [2,30] for examples) and interpolants (see [22] for a thorough overview) in SMT solving. Proofs serve as evidence of the correct solution to a problem and have become a crucial aspect of SMT solvers. The quality of proof depends on the solution path chosen by the solver, and CDCL-based approaches are expected to lead to better proofs as they generate more conflict clauses, providing more information for proof production. More conflict clauses also allow for the creation of more accurate interpolants, as additional constraints can be imposed on the system, reducing the set of possible assignments.

2   Preliminaries

Satisfiability modulo theories (SMT) solvers have shown to be particularly efficient in solving ground, multi-sorted first-order formulas with arithmetic. The input instance is interpreted as an arbitrary propositional formula over atoms that have Boolean truth values but may represent constraints in different theories, such as inequalities over arithmetic expressions, and equalities over uninterpreted functions defined over possibly uninterpreted sorts. The idea in SMT solving is to find a satisfying assignment or prove the absence of one by combining a solver for propositional satisfiability (SAT) with solvers for conjunctions of theory equalities and inequalities.

When this theory structure is ignored, the formula can be solved using a SAT solver. If a SAT solver finds a satisfying assignment, it represents a conjunction of equalities and inequalities appearing inside the atoms in the original formula. In the theory interpretation this conjunction might still be unsatisfiable, as the SAT solver could assign truth values for the equalities or inequalities that are inconsistent in the underlying theories. To overcome the problem, the theory solvers are queried for consistency of an assignment proposed by a SAT solver. In the case of unsatisfiability, the theory solvers provide an explanation for the unsatisfiability, expressed as a disjunction of theory atoms. The theory solver is allowed to not determine the satisfiability, in which case it provides new atoms for the SAT solver to branch on.

Modern SAT solvers work by gradually expanding a decision stack, that is, a truth assignment to the atoms of the instance. The stack can be extended either by branching on truth values of atoms or by unit propagation. The former is a heuristics process, whereas the latter works by finding clauses where under the current truth assignment exactly one literal is unassigned and all others are assigned to false and assigning the remaining literal to true. Unit propagation may terminate in a conflict, where a literal should be assigned simultaneously to true and false. This triggers a conflict analysis which aims at finding a point in the truth assignment where the solver should be backtracked to resolve the conflict. The analysis is a limited form of resolution and results in a *learned clause*, which is guaranteed to have all but one literal assigned false and the remaining literal unknown at the backtrack point. A pseudo-code for the satisfiability check within an SMT solver is given in Algorithm 1. The algorithm picks a literal for branching with heuristics (the call *bestLit()* on line 11) and runs unit propagation on line 2. If propagation ends in a conflict, either directly or as reported by a theory solver, the solver then adds a learned clause in line 5 and backtracks to a previous state in the decision stack.

The branching heuristics of an SMT solver has a big impact on solving efficiency. Literals are typically scored using an *activity-based heuristics* such as VSIDS [26], where atoms that appear often in the resolution receive higher scores. This is combined with an approach that tries to avoid creating immediate conflicts in the theories by preferring a polarity that is not conflicting with the model maintained internally by the theory solver.

An alternative to activity-based heuristics is the *lookahead heuristics* [17], which attempts at estimating the size of the remaining search space after branching by computing the number of unassigned atoms that would remain if an atom would be assigned. As a result of the theory explanations and the learned clauses, an SMT solver does not have a fixed number of clauses or even atoms. We may nevertheless use the number of unassigned atoms as an (inaccurate) proxy for the remaining search space size [15].

Algorithm 1: Basic CDCL algorithm.

	Input : An SMT instance in CNF ϕ;
	Output: SAT, UNSAT
	Data : Decision stack s, literal x_{best}
1	**while** *True* **do**
2	$\quad$ **while** *Propagate(s) results in conflict* **do**
3	$\quad\quad$ **if** *the decision level of s is 0* **then**
4	$\quad\quad\quad$ **return** UNSAT;
5	$\quad\quad$ $c \leftarrow$ analyse the conflict
6	$\quad\quad$ $\phi \leftarrow \phi \cup \{c\}$;
7	$\quad\quad$ Backtrack s until c becomes implying;
8	$\quad$ **end**
9	$\quad$ **if** $s \supseteq Var(\phi)$ **then**
10	$\quad\quad$ **return** SAT;
11	$\quad$ $x_{best} \leftarrow bestLit()$;
12	$\quad$ $s \leftarrow s \cdot (\{x_{best}\})$
13	**end**

Interpolation-Based Model Checking. Let $X = \{x_1, \ldots x_n\}$ be a set of variables in a multi-sorted logic and $X' = \{x' \mid x \in X\}$ a copy of these variables obtained by adding a prime in their symbols (used to represent the next state values of the variables). A transition system consisting of a set of initial states represented by $I(X)$,[1] a transition relation $Tr(X, X')$, and a safety property $P(X)$ that the system should satisfy. A typical task in a range of model-checking approaches is to first prove that a set of reachable states $J(X)$ cannot reach an error by showing the unsatisfiability of

$$J(X) \wedge Tr(X, X') \wedge \neg P(X), \tag{1}$$

and then generalising the set J to a safe super-set R, that is, $J(X) \rightarrow R(X)$, and $R(x) \wedge Tr(X, X') \rightarrow \neg P(X')$. Once obtained, the set R can for instance be studied for inductivity, i.e., whether $J(X) \wedge Tr(X, X') \rightarrow J(X')$. A range of techniques exists for obtaining the generalization R directly from the proof of unsatisfiability of (1) that an SMT solver produces almost as a side-product (see, e.g., [7,10,13]). The generalization R depends on the search, which in turn is guided by the branching heuristics. This observation will be at the center of our experimental evaluation of the lookahead-based techniques we study in this paper.

3   Picky CDCL

The Picky CDCL algorithm is based on the idea of creating a "more careful" version of VSIDS by incorporating a lookahead on top of it. This algorithm learns more clauses than VSIDS on each decision level, due to the wider scope of its propagations (as it tries to propagate ω variables at every round). Even in cases when no conflicts are encountered, this helps to guide VSIDS, because the literal which causes the most unit propagations is picked.

The implementation of this approach involves picking ω literals with the highest VSIDS score, propagating them, using CDCL(T)-style clause learning when conflicts are encountered during branching, calculating the maximal lookahead score, and branching on the literal with the highest score. In particular, as soon as a conflict is encountered when computing the lookahead, we learn the clause that will limit it in the future, and jump back to the second highest decision level of the literals in the learned clause. Algorithm 2 outlines the Picky CDCL algorithm.

The heuristics for deciding on literals is a straightforward enhancement of the VSIDS approach with two additional steps. The first is updating the VSIDS scores for the literals involved in the conflict analysis, which Picky CDLC does both on Line 5 during the "standard" propagation, and on Line 19 when a clause is learned in the lookahead phase. The second step implements the procedure that picks ω best literals with the highest VSIDS scores, instead of selecting just one best literal. The value ω is a parameter of the algorithm. It gives flexibility to Picky allowing it to pick between meticulous and quick approaches. Afterward,

---

[1] As is common, we identify a set S with the predicate $S(X)$ that evaluates to true on the elements of the set.

Algorithm 2: Picky CDCL algorithm.

    Input   : An SMT instance in CNF ϕ; search width ω;
    Output: SAT, UNSAT
    Data   : Decision stack s, literal x_{best}, map scores : $At(\phi) \rightarrow (\mathbb{N})$

1 **while** *True* **do**
2   **while** *Propagate(s) results in conflict* **do**
3   **if** *the decision level of s is 0* **then**
4 | **return** UNSAT;
5         $c \leftarrow$ analyse the conflict
6         $\phi \leftarrow \phi \cup \{c\}$;
7   Backtrack s until the second-highest decision level in c;
8   **end**
9   **if** $s \supseteq Var(\phi)$ **then**
10 | **return** SAT;
11     $x_{best} \leftarrow \top$;
        /* Resetting literal scores for the run of the lookahead   */
12     $scores[x] \leftarrow 0$ for all $x \in var(\phi)$;
13     $\kappa \leftarrow bestLits(\omega)$;
14   **for** *all $x \in \kappa$* **do**
        /* Push literal to the queue and propagate it to check the number of
           following unit propagations. Decision level is incremented at this
           point, and decremented during backtracking.   */
15         $s \leftarrow s \cdot (\{x\})$
16   **if** *Propagate(s) results in conflict* **then**
17   **if** *the decision level of s is 0* **then**
18 | **return** UNSAT;
19            $c \leftarrow$ analyse the conflict
20            $\phi \leftarrow \phi \cup \{c\}$;
21   Backtrack s until the second-highest decision level in c;
22   **goto** line 11;
23   **if** *CheckTheory() results in conflict* **then**
24 | **goto** line 16;
           /* la-score(x) returns a lookahead score for the literal   */
25         $scores[x] \leftarrow la\text{-}score(x)$;
26   **if** $scores[x] > scores[x_{best}]$ **then**
27 | $x_{best} \leftarrow x$;
28   Backtrack s until x becomes undefined;
29   **end**
        /* Best literal is picked for further propagation   */
31     $s \leftarrow s \cdot (\{x_{best}\})$;
32 **end**

Picky CDCL runs a lookahead algorithm for the picked literals, choosing the literal which will have the biggest impact on the propagation, i.e., the literal that, when fixed, causes the maximal amount of unit propagations as its consequence.

The main execution loop is on lines 1–31, as we propagate literals one by one and try to find a satisfiable literal assignment. On line 2 the current decision stack is propagated. Lines 3–7 manage the case where the propagation results in a conflict. If the solver is at decision level 0, the instance is trivially unsatisfiable. Otherwise, the solver needs to backtrack to the decision level at which conflict is mitigated (lines 5–7). Then, at line 9 we check if all of the variables were assigned, which means that the instance is satisfiable. The remaining part of the code is a heuristics to pick a literal for future propagation.

Picky CDCL starts by resetting x_{best} and literal scores in lines 11–12. On line 13, the ω best literals are selected based on the VSIDS heuristics and stored in a vector κ. This parameter can range from $\omega = 1$ to $\omega = nVars$, the total number of variables in the instance. The latter corresponds to running a full lookahead on every branching decision. The former is almost equivalent to the VSIDS heuristics, with small added overhead because of the second propagation[2]. The ability to control ω adds flexibility to the algorithm, as it allows to find a balance between performance (with smaller ω) and carefulness (with larger ω). Notably, ω is an input by the user of the solver and can be varied between different instances. In our experimentation, we observed that the value of ω should be picked carefully. Linear increase of the parameter ω may cause quadratic growth of the complexity because the ω number of literals are going to be propagated during each iteration of the Picky CDCL. In other words, the ω parameter is a breadth regulation of the search: it reduces the selection precision when it is decreased and increases the exploration space for the literal selection otherwise.

At lines 13–27 the Picky CDCL algorithm checks the propagations of all the literals in the vector κ, the literals with the highest VSIDS scores. Picky CDCL algorithm uses those literals to identify the one that will lead to the largest number of subsequent assignments through propagation, remembering the literal with the best result. In lines 16–21, Picky CDCL has another instance of conflict handling, as it may encounter conflicts during the "test" propagations. In case a conflict is encountered, Picky resets the lookahead scores and the best literals, because additional clauses were added and it may change scores for the literals. On line 23 Picky CDCL does a complete theory check, to validate that assignments are coherent with specific SMT theory. Due to this check, even Picky with $\omega = 1$ diverges in solution compared to the default VSIDS, catching conflicts earlier and producing more conflict clauses. Then, in the case of the successful propagation, at lines 24–27, Picky CDCL records the lookahead score and rolls back to the state before the test propagation of x.

Overall, the Picky CDCL algorithm can be described as an enhanced CDCL(T) with VSIDS. It incorporates CDCL(T) by allowing clause learning during propagation and expands the VSIDS heuristics by selecting the ω best literals and applying lookahead to them during literal selection. This approach provides more ways to find a solution and varies depending on the value of ω. Picky CDCL approach creates more clauses due to the use of clause learning,

---

[2] Propagation of the literal happens two times, on line 2, and line 15. It gives the capability to catch additional conflicts, but creates a slight overhead.

while still utilizing all of the VSIDS clauses. Therefore, compared to the classical VSIDS, Picky CDCL is expected to produce solutions more suitable for the applications that use interpolation-based SMT solving. We investigated this in our experimentation with the use of Picky CDCL in different applications (see Sect. 4).

4 Evaluation

The Picky CDCL algorithm was implemented on top of the interpolating SMT solver OpenSMT [9,19] with the production-ready versions of lookahead and VSIDS approaches. The solver works on quantifier-free logics of UF, LIA, and LRA, which provided a wide range of opportunities for experimentation with the new heuristics. We have experimented with the Picky CDCL and VSIDS algorithms.

This section provides an evaluation of our algorithm in the context of interpolation-based model checking and proof production. Main idea of the algorithm was to expand the applicability of SMT solving to better suit the verification tasks, therefore we experimented with the SMT-based model checking. We applied PickyCDCL for two applications: interpolation-based model checking (in CHC solver) and proof production/validation. Additionally, we evaluated the overhead of running Picky CDCL as compared to the classical VSIDS. All experiments were conducted with the optimizations on a machine with an AMD EPYC 7452 32-core processor and 8×32 GiB of memory. To test the Picky CDCL performance and application in the CHC solving we have used benchmark libraries from the CHC and SMT competitions. During experiments, no conflicts in the results were encountered.

4.1 Interpolation-Based Algorithms

The effect of the application of the Picky CDCL algorithm on interpolation-based reasoning was studied in the context of Constraint Horn Clauses solving. We experimented with Golem CHC solver [5] which integrates OpenSMT into its reasoning both for interpolation and solving. Golem is one of the most competitive CHC solvers (based on CHC-Comp 2023 and CHC-Comp 2022 [12]) and it supports a multitude of various interpolation-based verification algorithms such as Lazy Abstraction With Interpolants [25] (LAWI), Transition Power Abstraction [6] (TPA), Spacer [14] and Interpolation-based Model Checking [23] (IMC). Its architecture is displayed in Fig. 1. We experimented with three Golem's verification engines: TPA, LAWI, and Spacer, all of which used an OpenSMT solver with Picky CDCL and VSIDS heuristics as a backend for SMT solving. Next, we first give a brief overview of each CHC-solving approach used in our experimentation and then provide a comparative analysis for each of them with Picky CDCL and VSIDS-based backend engines.

LAWI is an algorithm that was introduced by McMillan for the verification of software. In the original description, the algorithm operates on programs represented with abstract reachability graphs, which map straightforwardly to linear CHC systems. This is the input supported by the implementation of the algorithm in Golem. Spacer is an IC3-based algorithm for solving general, even nonlinear, CHC systems. Nonlinear CHC systems can model programs with summaries, and in this setting, Spacer computes both under-approximating and over-approximating summaries of the procedures to achieve modular analysis of programs. Both in LAWI and Spacer interpolants play an important role. They are used to find safe state invariants that are used to prove system safety and allow to speed up the search of counter-examples. LAWI and Spacer can diverge while searching for inductive invariants if the SMT solver fails to produce suitable interpolants.

Unlike other interpolation-based engines like LAWI or Spacer, TPA [6] uses interpolants as abstractions over transitions, not states. Transition abstractions obtained from interpolants can significantly speed up the search for counter-examples as they allow to potentially prove safe all paths of a *range of lengths* with a single SMT query. Additionally, these interpolants serve as candidates for safe inductive *transition* invariants. Discovering such safe inductive transition invariant allows TPA to prove the transition system safe. The quality of the interpolants has a significant effect on the TPA's ability to solve the problem. TPA can spend a lot of time refining too coarse an abstraction, and it may never prove the system safe if the interpolants obtained from the SMT solver do not converge to an inductive transition invariant.

In our experimentation, we compared how the application of OpenSMT supporting Picky CDCL to Golem's TPA, Spacer, and LAWI verification engines affects their verification capabilities. In particular, we compared the number of instances solved by each verifier with OpenSMT's VSIDS and Picky CDCL core procedures. Furthermore, since Picky CDCL is flexible in the number of literals used for propagation (defined by parameter ω), in all our experiments we experimented with three instances of Picky CDCL. We used Picky CDCL with $\omega = 1$ (corresponding conceptually to the classical VSIDS algorithm), Picky CDCL with $\omega = nVars$ (corresponding conceptually to the classical lookahead), and the mixed Picky CDCL with ω being set to 10 (the choice of '10' was based on our empirical evaluation of various benchmarks[3]).

We performed an evaluation on two benchmark sets with LIA and LRA as the background theories. In particular, we focused on LRA-TS (497 tests) and LIA-lin (584 tests) sets from CHC-COMP [12], the benchmarks for which Golem had highly competitive performance results. In our experiments, we used an 1800 s timeout. The results are shown in Table 1. The number in the parenthesis is a number of uniquely solved instances, compared to the default SMT-solver engine, which is based on the VSIDS heuristics (listed first for each tool in the table).

---

[3] We observed on a wide range of the individual experiments that the ω parameter within a range between 10–20 provides the best CHC-solving performance for the Golem with Picky CDCL algorithm.

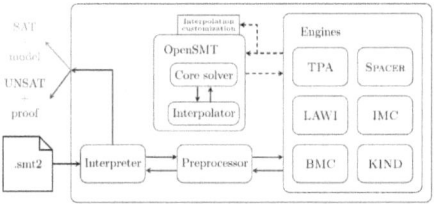

Fig. 1. An architecture of Golem CHC solver [5].

Our goal was to see that using the Picky CDCL algorithm, even though it may be slower than the core technique, would allow the verification engines to solve CHC instances that were not previously solvable using VSIDS. We also included the results for the DPLL lookahead [19] and tiebreaker [33] approaches, both of which were implemented in the OpenSMT solver.

Table 1. Golem results comparing various interpolation-based verification algorithms based on either VSIDS or Picky CDCL procedures of OpenSMT.

Algorithms	LIA-lin solved	LRA-TS solved
Number of benchmarks	585	498
TPA		
VSIDS	340	214
Picky CDCL with $\omega = 1$	338 (5)	202 (3)
Picky CDCL with $\omega = 10$	334 (7)	200 (6)
Picky CDCL with $\omega = nVars$	313 (2)	186 (5)
Lookahead DPLL	284 (1)	162
Tiebraker Lookahead	321 (5)	192 (5)
Spacer		
VSIDS	381	270
Picky CDCL with $\omega = 1$	379 (2)	270
Picky CDCL with $\omega = 10$	366 (2)	272 (2)
Picky CDCL with $\omega = nVars$	340	249
Lookahead DPLL	302	221
Tiebraker Lookahead	372 (1)	265 (1)
LAWI		
VSIDS	322	364
Picky CDCL with $\omega = 1$	315 (2)	358 (8)
Picky CDCL with $\omega = 10$	312 (3)	325 (10)
Picky CDCL with $\omega = nVars$	294 (3)	237
Lookahead DPLL	265 (2)	208
Tiebraker Lookahead	308 (2)	279 (3)

Overall, our comparative experimentation demonstrated that for most cases when the Picky CDCL algorithm was used, Golem was able to solve new unique instances which could not be solved while running the core procedures. While as expected, most of the time the core technique is able to solve more instances within the same timeout, the delay (see later for the overhead study) introduced by the Picky procedure corresponds only to a small reduction in the number of benchmarks being solved. Picky CDCL with $\omega = 1$ is able to solve unique instances compared to the VSIDS due to the divergence in the solving process, explained in Sect. 3. Interestingly, for Spacer, in one case for LRA-TS, it even solved more instances than the VSIDS procedure. Overall the results show that the mixed approach of Pickly CDCL is not only more flexible in its search because it enables it to solve previously unsolved benchmarks but it also naturally benefits from the performance efficiency of the classical algorithms since it remains comparable to the competitive algorithms used in our evaluation.

Random Tests. To illustrate that the effect of using Picky CDCL algorithm in Golem is not random, we conducted the following experiment with Golem, using the same set of LIA-lin and LRA-TS benchmarks as in the experiments above. We have created three instances of the VSIDS-based and three instances of the Picky-CDCL-based SMT solvers all with different random seeds. Then we ran them inside of the Golem CHC solver and produced a virtual portfolio of solved instances, where each portfolio consists of three Golem instances with different mixtures of the SMT backends. Table 2 summarizes the results of running the virtual portfolios. Notably, the portfolios which use the Picky CDCL approach are able to solve more instances overall. They systematically outperform the portfolios based solely on the VSIDS approach despite pure VSIDS being potentially more efficient.

Table 2. Virtual portfolios of TPA solving engines with different random seed. The limit is 3 engines per portfolio.

Virtual portfolio composition	LIA-lin solved	LRA-TS
3 VSIDS-based SMT solvers	345	223
2 VSIDS and 1 Picky-based SMT solvers	352	225
1 VSIDS and 2 Picky-based SMT solvers	354	230
3 Picky-based SMT solvers	343	220

We also closely examined some benchmarks (chosen randomly) which Golem uniquely solved using Picky-CDCL and reran them with ten instances of the VSIDS-based Golem with different random seeds. For example, *chc-LIA-Lin_325* was not solved by any of the random-seed Golem instances. Another example is a *chc-LIA-Lin_035* instance, that was solved by VSIDS-based Golem only 2 times out of 10. This shows that Picky-CDCL-based Golem can uniquely solve instances, disregarding the randomness. Overall, as confirmed by our extensive evaluation, the lookahead-inspired mixed approach for SMT solving allows for the potential discovery of shorter and more precise solutions better suitable for the verification tasks. It becomes a valuable component in the portfolio of proof-based interpolation model checking. Furthermore, as our experimentation with running a portfolio of the solutions suggests, Picky CDCL becomes a valuable tool for the purposes of CHC-solving if run as a part of a portfolio.

4.2   Proof Production

Another set of experiments was conducted with OpenSMT's proof production and proof validation engine. Proofs are an important part of any modern SAT/SMT solver because they allow to validate the correctness of unsatisfiability results, showing that the solver did not deviate. OpenSMT supports proof production using the VSIDS SMT solving procedure [19]. We adopted OpenSMT to support the proof production using the Picky CDCL algorithm instead. OpenSMT produces proofs in the DRAT format and we evaluated the effect of using the Picky CDCL as compared to the VSIDS approach by investigating its effect on the proof size and the proof validation time.

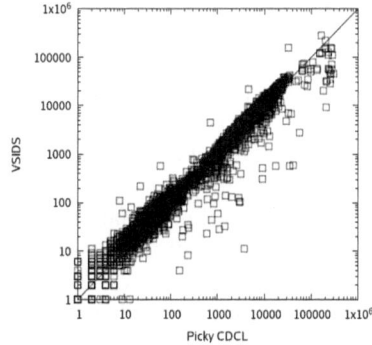

Fig. 2. A comparison of proof size for the VSIDS approach vs the Picky CDCL. (In the number of unique lemmas used)

The proof size was estimated by measuring the number of employed lemmas in the corresponding formulae. We conducted a series of experiments for QF UF benchmarks taken from SMT-comp [3]. Overall, we evaluated 1752 tests with 1200 s time limit, all of which demonstrated a similar trend. The results show that the proofs produced by OpenSMT with the Picky CDCL backend on average have 15% more lemmas than proofs produced by the core solver technique. This can be connected with the fact that the Picky CDCL procedure produces 2–3 times more clauses while executing the solving, therefore extending the possible picks of lemmas for the proof production. The results for OpenSMT based on the VSIDS and Picky CDCL are shown in Fig. 2.

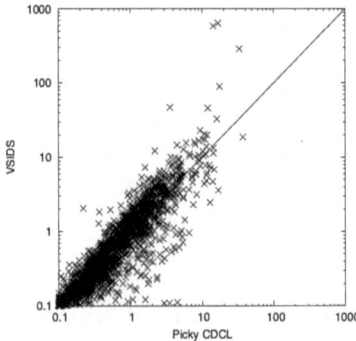

Fig. 3. A comparison of the validation time for VSIDS built proofs against the Picky-CDCL-built proofs. (Time comparison in seconds)

We also conducted a comparison between the time it took to validate proofs produced from the QF UF benchmarks, which were solved both by the VSIDS-based and Picky CDCL-based solvers with 1000 s timeout. The latter was expected to be able to create more optimal proof routes, or at least the same ones as the VSIDS-based OpenSMT, thanks to the additional clauses produced as a result of the detected conflicts. DRAT-trim [16,32] tool was used to validate the proof results. The results can be seen in Fig. 3.

The graph data shows that the proof validation process for the Picky CDCL-based solver proofs was faster compared to the validation process for proofs produced by the VSIDS-based solver. The Y-axis on the graph represents the time for the VSIDS-produced proof to be validated, and the X-axis stands for the time for the Picky CDCL proof to be validated. It was found that the Picky CDCL proof validation only took 2475.49 s, whereas the VSIDS validation was significantly slower with 4203.87 s. This implies that the Picky CDCL was able to create proofs that are easier to validate[4]. Therefore Picky CDCL can be used in a portfolio for proof-based interpolation in model checking with a positive effect.

4.3 Overhead Evaluation

The mixed approach proposed for the flexible literal selection of the Picky CDCL procedure naturally requires more computational resources than the core VSIDS approach. We studied the overhead of the combined approach for OpenSMT on the SMT-comp benchmarks for QF LRA, the same ones as were used for Proof production evaluation. The comparison used the Picky CDCL implementation with different values of the ω parameter ($\omega = nVars$, $\omega = 10$, and $\omega = 1$). The timeout for the SMT solving was set to 1200 s. Overall, we noticed that the increase of the ω leads to a more significant performance overhead, for $\omega = nVars$

---

[4] The solver may be selecting suboptimal clauses during its solving process which could be the cause of points below the median line.

performance slowdown compared to the VSIDS was the same as for the full lookahead approach. This is happens due to the increased number of literal propagations in case of increased ω (because of growth of number of considered picks).

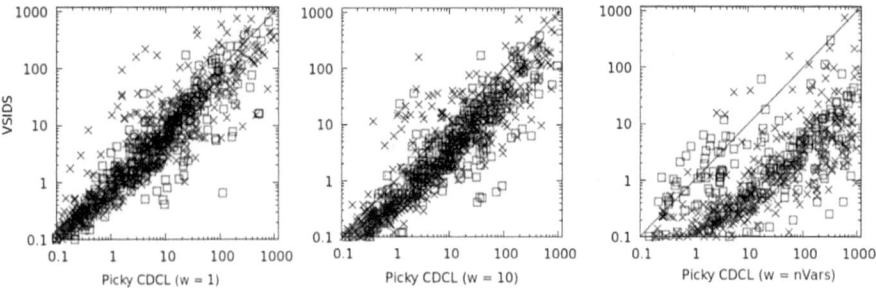

Fig. 4. Overhead evaluation for OpenSMT with Picky CDCL-based vs VSIDS-based solving for various depths of literal selection. (Time comparison in seconds)

Figure 4 illustrates the comparison of the Picky CDCL with the VSIDS for the cases of $\omega = 1$, $\omega = 10$, and $\omega = n\text{Vars}$. Crosses on the graph mean SAT, squares UNSAT results. Noticeably, Picky CDCL with $\omega = 1$ is slower by a factor of 1.3 compared to VSIDS, due to the reasons explained in Sect. 3. Picky CDCL with $\omega = 10$ is on average 1.81 times slower than VSIDS, even though it propagates ten times more literals at each decision round and finds 2–3 times more conflicts, than the classical VSIDS approach. As such, we can conclude that the algorithm became significantly faster than the lookahead approach, especially with the smaller ω, but is still able to find significantly more information about the instance (learned clauses), in comparison with VSIDS.

4.4   Lookahead Comparison

Picky CDCL heuristics was developed as a mixed approach combining VSIDS and lookahead strategies. Both of those techniques were implemented in OpenSMT [20] prior to our development of Picky CDCL. Lookahead in OpenSMT is based on the DPLL procedure, which was developed for the purpose of splitting SMT solving in the context of parallel reasoning. During the development of the DPLL-based lookahead in parallel OpenSMT, the performance of solving was secondary, because it was developed for efficient distribution of reasoning. As a result, lookahead is slower compared to the standard VSIDS heuristics. Since both lookahead and Picky CDCL are implemented in the same tool, we compared their performance. Implementations of heuristics are orthogonal since the lookahead procedure is based on DPLL, and Picky CDCL is based on a pure CDCL engine. Picky CDCL technique was executed with different ω coefficients ($\omega = n\text{Vars}$, $\omega = 10$, and $\omega = 1$). The results of the Picky CDCL and lookahead comparison are presented in Fig. 5.

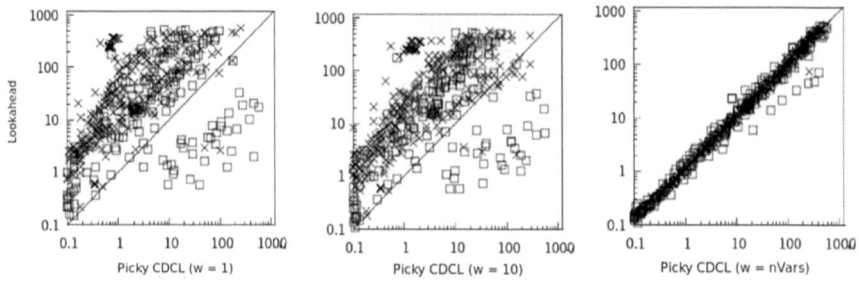

Fig. 5. Picky CDCL-based vs lookahead-based OpenSMT performance comparison for various depths of literal selection. (Time comparison in seconds)

As expected, Picky CDCL with smaller ω turned out to be significantly faster than the lookahead approach, for example, Picky CDCL with $\omega = 10$ is 8 times faster than the lookahead. And for $\omega = n\,Vars$, the Picky CDCL approach turned out to be as productive as the lookahead technique. Therefore, performance-wise we can conclude that Picky CDCL can outperform the lookahead technique, and it doesn't lose to it even for the maximal value of ω.

5   Conclusions

Most research projects in SAT/SMT solving prioritize performance when developing and improving solvers. Faster execution times and the capacity to analyze complex tasks can greatly enhance the possibilities of these solvers. However, in the pursuit of speed, practical applications of the tools can be neglected. This paper investigated how lookahead-inspired SMT solving, when made sufficiently efficient and integrated into a conflict-driven clause learning SMT core, can be a valuable component in a portfolio for proof-based interpolation in model checking.

We implemented the algorithmic idea called Picky CDCL in the OpenSMT solver and showed its efficiency in application to the interpolation-based algorithms (using Golem) and SMT proof validation. Overall, this approach demonstrates that more careful methods can yield better outcomes for specific cases. Through our extensive experimentation with the Picky CDCL-based solver, we observed that it was able to solve unique instances of CHC benchmarks that were not solved by the classical VSIDS, and produced proofs that were easier to validate. The study of the overhead cost of our procedure demonstrates that it is minimal and can be parameterized by the selection of literals, maintaining the efficiency of the search.

The results of this study demonstrate that while the pursuit of the most performant approach is a powerful method, practical results often benefit from slower, steadier progress. For practical applications, it is thus beneficial to include a few solving algorithms that can cover the entirety of the solution area, thus increasing the tool's overall solving capabilities.

As future work, we plan to optimize Picky CDCL using chronological back-tracking [28], which will significantly decrease the rollback of the solver during conflict resolution. This would significantly increase the speed of the algorithm.

References

1. Alt, L., Fedyukovich, G., Hyvärinen, A.E.J., Sharygina, N.: A proof-sensitive app-roach for small propositional interpolants. In: Gurfinkel, A., Seshia, S.A. (eds.) VSTTE 2015. LNCS, vol. 9593, pp. 1–18. Springer, Cham (2016). https://doi.org/10.1007/978-3-319-29613-5_1

2. Barbosa, H., et al.: Flexible proof production in an industrial-strength SMT solver. In: Blanchette, J., Kovács, L., Pattinson, D. (eds.) Proceedings of the 11th International Joint Conference on Automated Reasoning, IJCAR 2022, Haifa, Israel, 8–10 August 2022. LNCS, vol. 13385, pp. 15–35. Springer, Heidelberg (2022). https://doi.org/10.1007/978-3-031-10769-6_3

3. Barrett, C., de Moura, L., Stump, A.: SMT-COMP: satisfiability modulo theories competition. In: Etessami, K., Rajamani, S.K. (eds.) CAV 2005. LNCS, vol. 3576, pp. 20–23. Springer, Heidelberg (2005). https://doi.org/10.1007/11513988_4

4. Barrett, C., Nieuwenhuis, R., Oliveras, A., Tinelli, C.: Splitting on demand in SAT modulo theories. In: Hermann, M., Voronkov, A. (eds.) LPAR 2006. LNCS (LNAI), vol. 4246, pp. 512–526. Springer, Heidelberg (2006). https://doi.org/10.1007/11916277_35

5. Blicha, M., Britikov, K., Sharygina, N.: The GOLEM Horn solver. In: Enea, C., Lal, A. (eds.) Computer Aided Verification, CAV 2023. LNCS, vol. 13965, pp. 209–223. Springer, Cham (2023). https://doi.org/10.1007/978-3-031-37703-7_10

6. Blicha, M., Fedyukovich, G., Hyvärinen, A.E.J., Sharygina, N.: Split transition power abstraction for unbounded safety. In: Griggio, A., Rungta, N. (eds.) 22nd Formal Methods in Computer-Aided Design, FMCAD 2022, Trento, Italy, 17–21 October 2022, pp. 349–358. IEEE (2022). https://doi.org/10.34727/2022/isbn.978-3-85448-053-2_42

7. Blicha, M., Hyvärinen, A.E.J., Kofroň, J., Sharygina, N.: Decomposing Farkas interpolants. In: Vojnar, T., Zhang, L. (eds.) TACAS 2019, Part I. LNCS, vol. 11427, pp. 3–20. Springer, Cham (2019). https://doi.org/10.1007/978-3-030-17462-0_1

8. Böhm, M., Speckenmeyer, E.: A fast parallel SAT-solver - efficient workload balancing. Ann. Math. Artif. Intell. **17**, 381–400 (1996). https://doi.org/10.1007/BF02127976

9. Bruttomesso, R., Pek, E., Sharygina, N., Tsitovich, A.: The OpenSMT solver. In: Esparza, J., Majumdar, R. (eds.) TACAS 2010. LNCS, vol. 6015, pp. 150–153. Springer, Heidelberg (2010). https://doi.org/10.1007/978-3-642-12002-2_12

10. Craig, W.: Three uses of the Herbrand-Gentzen theorem in relating model theory and proof theory. J. Symb. Log. **22**, 269–285 (1957). https://doi.org/10.2307/2963594

11. Davis, M., Logemann, G., Loveland, D.W.: A machine program for theorem-proving. Commun. ACM **5**, 394–397 (1962). https://doi.org/10.1145/368273.368557

12. De Angelis, E., Hari Govind, V.K.: CHC-COMP 2022: competition report. In: Hamilton, G.W., Kahsai, T., Proietti, M. (eds.) Proceedings 9th Workshop on Horn Clauses for Verification and Synthesis and 10th International Workshop on Verification and Program Transformation, HCVS/VPT@ETAPS 2022 and 10th International Workshop on Verification and Program Transformation, Munich, Germany, 3 April 2022, EPTCS, vol. 373, pp. 44–62 (2022). https://doi.org/10.4204/EPTCS.373.5
13. D'Silva, V.: Propositional interpolation and abstract interpretation. In: Gordon, A.D. (ed.) ESOP 2010. LNCS, vol. 6012, pp. 185–204. Springer, Heidelberg (2010). https://doi.org/10.1007/978-3-642-11957-6_11
14. Gurfinkel, A.: Program verification with constrained horn clauses (invited paper). In: Shoham, S., Vizel, Y. (eds.) Proceedings of the 34th International Conference on Computer Aided Verification, CAV 2022, Part I. LNCS, Haifa, Israel, 7–10 August 2022, vol. 13371, pp. 19–29. Springer, Heidelberg (2022). https://doi.org/10.1007/978-3-031-13185-1_2
15. Heule, M.J.H., Kullmann, O., Wieringa, S., Biere, A.: Cube and conquer: guiding CDCL SAT solvers by lookaheads. In: Eder, K., Lourencco, J., Shehory, O. (eds.) HVC 2011. LNCS, vol. 7261, pp. 50–65. Springer, Heidelberg (2012). https://doi.org/10.1007/978-3-642-34188-5_8
16. Heule, M.J.H.: The DRAT format and drat-trim checker. CoRR abs/1610.06229 (2016)
17. Heule, M.J.H., van Maaren, H.: Look-ahead based SAT solvers, 2nd edn. In: Biere, A., Heule, M., van Maaren, H., Walsh, T. (eds.) Handbook of Satisfiability, Frontiers in Artificial Intelligence and Applications, vol. 336, pp. 183–212. IOS Press (2021). https://doi.org/10.3233/FAIA200988
18. Hojjat, H., Rümmer, P.: The ELDARICA horn solver. In: Bjørner, N.S., Gurfinkel, A. (eds.) 2018 Formal Methods in Computer Aided Design, FMCAD 2018, Austin, TX, USA, 30 October–2 November 2018, pp. 1–7. IEEE (2018). https://doi.org/10.23919/FMCAD.2018.8603013
19. Hyvärinen, A.E.J., Marescotti, M., Alt, L., Sharygina, N.: OpenSMT2: an SMT solver for multi-core and cloud computing. In: Creignou, N., Le Berre, D. (eds.) SAT 2016. LNCS, vol. 9710, pp. 547–553. Springer, Cham (2016). https://doi.org/10.1007/978-3-319-40970-2_35
20. Hyvärinen, A.E.J., Marescotti, M., Sadigova, P., Chockler, H., Sharygina, N.: Lookahead-based SMT solving. In: Barthe, G., Sutcliffe, G., Veanes, M. (eds.) 22nd International Conference on Logic for Programming, Artificial Intelligence and Reasoning, LPAR-22. EPiC Series in Computing, Awassa, Ethiopia, 16–21 November 2018, vol. 57, pp. 418–434. EasyChair (2018). https://doi.org/10.29007/gzzf
21. Komuravelli, A., Gurfinkel, A., Chaki, S.: SMT-based model checking for recursive programs. Formal Meth. Syst. Des. **48**, 175–205 (2016). https://doi.org/10.1007/s10703-016-0249-4
22. Konnov, I.: Edmund M. Clarke, Thomas A. Henzinger, Helmut Veith, and Roderick Bloem (eds):Handbook of model checking. Formal Aspects Comput. **31**(4), 455–456 (2019). https://doi.org/10.1007/s00165-019-00486-z
23. McMillan, K.L.: Interpolation and SAT-based model checking. In: Hunt, W.A., Somenzi, F. (eds.) CAV 2003. LNCS, vol. 2725, pp. 1–13. Springer, Heidelberg (2003). https://doi.org/10.1007/978-3-540-45069-6_1
24. McMillan, K.L.: Applications of Craig interpolants in model checking. In: Halbwachs, N., Zuck, L.D. (eds.) TACAS 2005. LNCS, vol. 3440, pp. 1–12. Springer, Heidelberg (2005). https://doi.org/10.1007/978-3-540-31980-1_1

25. McMillan, K.L.: Lazy abstraction with interpolants. In: Ball, T., Jones, R.B. (eds.) CAV 2006. LNCS, vol. 4144, pp. 123–136. Springer, Heidelberg (2006). https://doi.org/10.1007/11817963_14

26. Moskewicz, M.W., Madigan, C.F., Zhao, Y., Zhang, L., Malik, S.: Chaff: engineering an efficient SAT solver. In: Proceedings of the 38th Design Automation Conference, DAC 2001, Las Vegas, NV, USA, 18–22 June 2001, pp. 530–535. ACM (2001). https://doi.org/10.1145/378239.379017

27. de Moura, L., Bjørner, N.: Z3: an efficient SMT solver. In: Ramakrishnan, C.R., Rehof, J. (eds.) TACAS 2008. LNCS, vol. 4963, pp. 337–340. Springer, Heidelberg (2008). https://doi.org/10.1007/978-3-540-78800-3_24

28. Nadel, A., Ryvchin, V.: Chronological backtracking. In: Beyersdorff, O., Wintersteiger, C.M. (eds.) SAT 2018. LNCS, vol. 10929, pp. 111–121. Springer, Cham (2018). https://doi.org/10.1007/978-3-319-94144-8_7

29. Oh, C.: Between SAT and UNSAT: the fundamental difference in CDCL SAT. In: Heule, M., Weaver, S. (eds.) SAT 2015. LNCS, vol. 9340, pp. 307–323. Springer, Cham (2015). https://doi.org/10.1007/978-3-319-24318-4_23

30. Otoni, R., Blicha, M., Eugster, P., Hyvärinen, A.E.J., Sharygina, N.: Theory-specific proof steps witnessing correctness of SMT executions. In: 58th ACM/IEEE Design Automation Conference, DAC 2021, San Francisco, CA, USA, 5–9 December 2021, pp. 541–546. IEEE (2021). https://doi.org/10.1109/DAC18074.2021.9586272

31. Silva, J.P.M., Sakallah, K.A.: Conflict analysis in search algorithms for satisfiability. In: Eigth International Conference on Tools with Artificial Intelligence, ICTAI '96, Toulouse, France, 16–19 November 1996, pp. 467–469. IEEE Computer Society (1996). https://doi.org/10.1109/TAI.1996.560789

32. Wetzler, N., Heule, M.J.H., Hunt, W.A.: DRAT-trim: efficient checking and trimming using expressive clausal proofs. In: Sinz, C., Egly, U. (eds.) SAT 2014. LNCS, vol. 8561, pp. 422–429. Springer, Cham (2014). https://doi.org/10.1007/978-3-319-09284-3_31

33. Xiao, F., Li, C.-M., Luo, M., Manyà, F., Lü, Z., Li, Yu.: A branching heuristic for SAT solvers based on complete implication graphs. Sci. China Inf. Sci. **62**(7), 72103:1-72103:13 (2019). https://doi.org/10.1007/s11432-017-9467-7

Safety Performance of Neural Networks in the Presence of Covariate Shift

Chih-Hong Cheng[1,2]([✉]), Harald Ruess[3], and Konstantinos Theodorou[1]

[1] Fraunhofer IKS, Munich, Germany
{chih-hong.cheng,konstantinos.theodorou}@iks.fraunhofer.de
[2] University of Hildesheim, Hildesheim, Germany
[3] Fortiss GmbH, Munich, Germany
ruess@fortiss.org

Abstract. Covariate shift may impact the operational safety performance of neural networks. A re-evaluation of the safety performance, however, requires collecting new operational data and creating corresponding ground truth labels, which often is not possible during operation. We are therefore proposing to reshape the initial test set, as used for the safety performance evaluation prior to deployment, based on an approximation of the operational data. This approximation is obtained by observing and learning the distribution of activation patterns of neurons in the network during operation. The reshaped test set reflects the distribution of neuron activation values as observed during operation, and may therefore be used for re-evaluating safety performance in the presence of covariate shift. First, we derive conservative bounds on the values of neurons by applying finite binning and static dataflow analysis. Second, we formulate a *mixed integer linear programming* (MILP) constraint for constructing the minimum set of data points to be removed in the test set, such that the difference between the discretized test and operational distributions is bounded. We discuss potential benefits and limitations of this constraint-based approach based on our initial experience with an implemented research prototype.

Keywords: distribution reshaping · machine learning · MILP · performance estimation

1 Introduction

Covariate shift in machine-learned systems occurs when the input distribution changes between training and operation stages [14]. This phenomenon is present in most applications of machine learning, as training sets usually do not sufficiently reflect the complexity of real-world operational contexts and their potential changes. This kind of dataset shift is also a major concern in transfer learning when exposing machine-learned systems to solving different tasks [8].

There is a fundamental dichotomy between covariate shift of machine-learned systems during operation and their underlying safety requirements, which require demonstrating given *safety performance indicators* (SPIs) [1,7] prior to deployment. The challenge we are tackling therefore is to incorporate the possibility

A. Reynolds and S. Tasiran (Eds.): VSTTE 2023, LNCS 14095, pp. 20–30, 2024.
https://doi.org/10.1007/978-3-031-66064-1_2

of operational covariate shift into safety assurance arguments for safety-related neural networks. Hereby, we assume that the initial test data for SPI evaluation is known but the operational data is unknown, since collecting operational data and creating corresponding ground truth labels is usually not possible during operation.

In tackling this challenge, we develop a specialized online monitoring technique for estimating the change of values of SPIs due to covariate shift. For practical purposes, we restrict ourselves to feed-forward deep neural networks (DNN), and we assume that the values of monitored neurons (in the feature space) of this DNN adequately reflect the input data distribution. Now, for each monitored neuron, one constructs the histogram of distributions based on binning, and distribution shift is observed by comparing the shape of two such histograms. Such information abstracts the details of the observed input in operation, thereby bypassing practical limitations where arbitrarily initiating a data collection regime when the DNN is integrated into an application has technical and societal constraints. One of our measures of similarity, called κ-KL similarity, is inspired by the Kullback-Leibler divergence. The purpose of a second measure, called ϵ-portion similarity, is to characterize bounded differences. Key to our approach is that SPI estimations are reduced to constructing a subset of the test data that matches the similarity measure demonstrated by the operation, followed by the recomputation of the SPI on this subset. For ϵ-portion similarity, when the input is of bounded range we introduce a *mixed integer linear programming* (MILP) encoding with 0–1 variables, whereby an upper limit on the number of bins can be obtained from static dataflow analyis.

In Sect. 2 we review and compare with most closely related work. Section 3 defines ϵ-portion similarity for measuring the similarity of distributions based on neuron activations. Next, Sect. 4 describes distribution reshaping for ϵ-portion similarity via test set reduction together its encoding in MILP. This algorithm is evaluated in Sect. 5 based on standard machine learning benchmarks, and we conclude in Sect. 6 with discussing the potential benefits and current limitations of our approach.

2   Related Work

The divergence between a source and a target distribution, as obtained, say, by dataset shift is usually measured in terms of *mutual information* or KL divergence [14]. Unfortunately, measuring mutual information from finite data is a notoriously difficult estimation problem [4,9], and there are statistical limitations on measuring lower bounds on KL divergence from finite data [12]. Since our techniques are intended to be applied during operation, we are therefore measuring covariate shift only indirectly by observing and comparing abstracted distributions on corresponding neuronal excitements. This kind of indirect measurement does not require the original detailed operational data (e.g., images) to be available.

Covariate shift in machine-learned systems may be corrected using, say, *weighted empirical risk minimization* [16], which is based on retraining the system with a calibrated loss function based on the ratio of source and the target distribution of inputs. Retraining of safety-related machine-learned components, however, is problematic, and the best we can do is to adequately measure the potential drop of relevant safety performance indicators which are due to covariate shift. This implies that when data in operation is only made available as abstracted distributions, we need to reshape the test data to create an estimation. ϵ-portion similarity, as developed here, is to practically consider the non-linearity caused by KL-divergence as the similarity measure, thereby enabling a reduction to MILP.

Within the research field of safe autonomous driving, *leading measures* [3] are proactive indicators that assess prevention efforts and can be observed and evaluated before a crash occurs. Our approach to SPI re-estimation under distribution reshaping yields a leading measure on the level of a machine-learned component. Our developments also go beyond *out-of-distribution* techniques for detecting outliers with respect to training inputs [11,15], as we are constructing an aggregated SPI against all observed data, where even when every data point being observed in operation is *within-distribution*, this does not imply that the SPI will be the same.

3   Distribution Similarity Based on Neuron Values

$\mathcal{D}_{op}$ denotes the multiset of data points, which are collected during operation, and $\mathcal{D}_{test}$ is the multiset of data points used in the (safety) performance evaluation. We assume as given a feed-forward *deep neural network* (DNN) $F \overset{\text{def}}{=} f^L \circ \ldots \circ f^1$, which is composed of layers 1 through L. Each *layer* l_i is a function $\mathbb{R}^{d_{i-1}} \to \mathbb{R}^{d_i}$, with d_i the dimensions of vectors. Layers consists of a set of neurons for computing a weighted linear sum from the input of the previous layer, followed by applying some monotonically non-decreasing activation function, such as *ReLU*, *Leaky ReLU*, and *tanh*. Without loss of generality, the neurons in F are fully connected with subsequent layers. The notation $l_A \in \{1, \ldots, L\}$ indicates the chosen layer for analyzing distribution similarity between $\mathcal{D}_{op}$ and $\mathcal{D}_{test}$. For a data point in, the output at the l-th layer is the vector $F^l(\text{in}) := f^l(f^{l-1}(\ldots f^1(\text{in})))$ of dimension d_l. Now, $F_i^l(\text{in})$ projects the i-th output from $F^l(\text{in})$, and f_i^l is the output of the i-th neuron at the l-th layer; that is, given an input in, f_i^l takes $F^{l-1}(\text{in})$ as input and produces $f_i^l(F^{l-1}(\text{in}))$ which equals $F_i^l(\text{in})$. Finally, all inputs are bounded by an interval $[v_{min}, v_{max}]$, where v_{min}, v_{max} are fixed constants. In other words, in $\in [v_{min}, v_{max}]^{d_0}$ and $\mathcal{D}_{op}, \mathcal{D}_{test} \subseteq [v_{min}, v_{max}]^{d_0}$. For a multiset $\mathcal{D}$ of data points and given DNN F, we define

$$V_i^l(\mathcal{D}) \overset{\text{def}}{=} \langle F_i^l(\text{in}) \mid \text{in} \in \mathcal{D} \rangle \tag{1}$$

to be the multiset of all values of the i-th neuron value at layer l for all inputs in $\mathcal{D}$.

Definition 1. *For a natural number $N > 0$, a positive real number Δ and a real number $c \in \mathbb{R}$, the (c, Δ, N)-**binning function** $b_N^{c,\Delta} : [c, c + (N+1)\Delta] \rightarrow \{0, 1, \dots, N\}$ is defined as follows:*

$$b_N^{c,\Delta}(x) = \begin{cases} 0 & \text{if } x \in [c, c + \Delta] \\ j & \text{else if } x \in (c + j\Delta, c + (j+1)\Delta], \text{ for any } j \in \{1, \dots, N\} \end{cases} \tag{2}$$

We apply each element in $V_i^{l_A}(\mathcal{D}_{op})$ with a binning function in order to derive another multiset

$$B_i^{l_A}(F, \mathcal{D}_{op}) \overset{\text{def}}{=} \langle b_N^{c,\Delta}(F_i^{l_A}(\text{in})) \mid \text{in} \in \mathcal{D}_{op}\rangle. \tag{3}$$

This requires, however, that for all in $\in \mathcal{D}_{op}$, $F_i^{l_A}(\text{in}) \in [c, c+(N+1)\Delta]$. Provided that any input is bounded where in $\in [v_{min}, v_{max}]^{d_o}$, we have the following property.

Lemma 1. *Let Δ be a positive constant. Provided that $\mathcal{D}_{op}, \mathcal{D}_{test} \subseteq [v_{min}, v_{max}]^{d_o}$ and F is implemented layer-wise with each neuron f_i^l implemented by (1) performing a weighted linear sum from the previous layer, followed by (2) applying monotonically non-decreasing computational activation function, there exists a constant $c \in \mathbb{R}$ and $N \in \mathbb{N}$ such that for all $i \in \{1, \dots, d_l\}$, $F_i^{l_A}(\text{in}) \in [c, c + N\Delta]$, where c and N can be computed in time linear to the number of neurons.*

Proof. (Sketch) This is based on the known result in neural network verification using abstract interpretation [2,5,6], where provided that input is bounded, and F is implemented with (1) and (2), one can apply computationally efficient interval-bound propagation (boxed abstraction) [2,6] to derive a conservative minimum and maximum bound $[v_{i,min}, v_{i,max}]$ such that $\{F_i^{l_A}(\text{in}) \mid \text{in} \in [v_{min}, v_{max}]^{d_o}\} \subseteq [v_{i,min}, v_{i,max}]$, where the interval-bound analysis is done in time linear to the total amount of neurons (see Example 1 for illustration).[1] With the following value assignment for c and N, the lemma then holds.

$$c := \min(v_{1,min}, \dots, v_{d_l,min}) \tag{4}$$

$$N := \left\lceil \frac{\max(v_{1,max}, \dots, v_{d_l,max}) - c}{\Delta} \right\rceil \tag{5}$$

$\square$

Example 1. Consider the example in Fig. 1, where we wish to perform the analysis at layer $l_A = 2$. Assume $\Delta = 3$, and for each input at the left, it has the domain $[-1, 1]$, i.e., $\mathcal{D}_{op}, \mathcal{D}_{test} \subseteq [-1, 1]^3$. For each neuron $(f_1^1, f_2^1, f_1^2, f_2^2)$, its computation is completed by first performing a weighted sum (the corresponding weight is attached in the edge) followed by the nonlinear activation ReLU

---

[1] This is because intuitively, a deep neural network is nothing different than a program without loop. Therefore, interval-bound propagation only requires a single pass.

$(ReLU(x) \overset{\text{def}}{:=} \max(0,x))$. The result of interval-bound propagation provides us a conservative estimate $v_{1,min} = v_{2,min} = 0$, $v_{1,max} = 14$, $v_{2,max} = 5$. Therefore, $c = \min(0,0) = 0$ and $N = \lceil \frac{\max(14,5)-0}{3} \rceil = 5$.

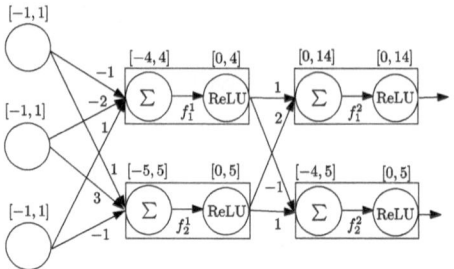

Fig. 1. An example of using bound propagation to conservatively estimate c and N.

Table 1. Comparing two distribution similarity measures

Distribution similarity	Sensitive to $|\mathcal{D}_{op}|$	Non-emptiness in bin	Dist. reshaping via MILP
κ-KL similar	no	needed	no
ϵ-portion similar	no	not needed	yes

By applying each element in $V_i^{l_A}(\mathcal{D}_{op})$ with the binning function created using Lemma 1, one derives another multiset $B_i^{l_A}(F, \mathcal{D}_{op}) \overset{\text{def}}{:=} \langle b_N^{c,\Delta}(F_i^{l_A}(\text{in})) \mid \text{in} \in \mathcal{D}_{op}\rangle$. Analogously, define $B_i^{l_A}(F, \mathcal{D}_{test})$ to abbreviate $\langle b_N^{c,\Delta}(F_i^{l_A}(\text{in})) \mid \text{in} \in \mathcal{D}_{test}\rangle$. Let $ct(j, \mathcal{D})$ be the function that counts the number of elements in multiset $\mathcal{D}$ having value j, and $|\mathcal{D}|$ returns the size of the multiset. We now define two types of distribution similarity.

Definition 2. *Given a positive constant κ, define $\mathcal{D}_{op}$ and $\mathcal{D}_{test}$ to be κ-KL similar (subject to DNN F, layer index l_A, and binning function $b_N^{c,\Delta}$), if:*

$$\forall i \in \{1,\ldots,d_l\} \quad : \quad \sum_{j=0}^{N} \frac{ct(j, B_i^{l_A}(F, \mathcal{D}_{test}))}{|\mathcal{D}_{test}|} \ln \frac{\frac{ct(j, B_i^{l_A}(F, \mathcal{D}_{test}))}{|\mathcal{D}_{test}|}}{\frac{ct(j, B_i^{l_A}(F, \mathcal{D}_{op}))}{|\mathcal{D}_{op}|}} \leq \kappa \quad (6)$$

Definition 3. *Given a positive constant ϵ, define $\mathcal{D}_{op}$ and $\mathcal{D}_{test}$ to be ϵ-portion similar (subject to DNN F, layer index l_A, and binning function $b_N^{c,\Delta}$) if:*

$$\forall i \in \{1,\ldots,d_l\}, \forall j \in \{0,\ldots,N\} :$$

$$-\epsilon \leq \frac{ct(j, B_i^{l_A}(F, \mathcal{D}_{op}))}{|\mathcal{D}_{op}|} - \frac{ct(j, B_i^{l_A}(F, \mathcal{D}_{test}))}{|\mathcal{D}_{test}|} \leq \epsilon \quad (7)$$

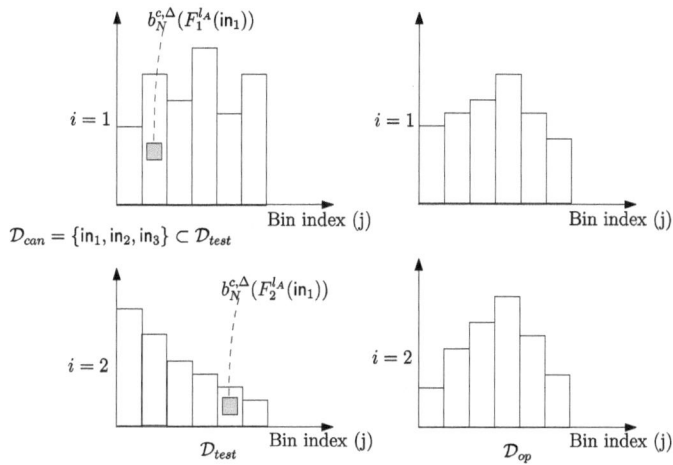

Fig. 2. Shaping the test set by removing or adding data points requires simultaneously considering the effect of multiple neurons. For example, although removing in_1 can reduce the count in bin $j = 2$ for $i = 1$, it may also undesirably reduce the count in bin $j = 4$ for $i = 2$. The counts in the Y-axis are not on the same scale but only show the tendency.

Table 1 summarizes the characteristics of our proposed distribution similarity measures. The definition of κ-KL similarity is based on the well-known definition of KL-divergence in a discrete setting. As the computation $\frac{\text{ct}(j, B_i^{l_A}(F, \mathcal{D}_{test}))}{|\mathcal{D}_{test}|}$ and $\frac{\text{ct}(j, B_i^{l_A}(F, \mathcal{D}_{op}))}{|\mathcal{D}_{op}|}$ are only the relative frequencies in appearing to a particular bin, it is not sensitive to the size of $\mathcal{D}_{op}$. Nevertheless, due to the nonlinear logarithm function in the definition, the distribution shaping problem with minimum data point removal naturally cannot be formulated using MILP, which is in contrast to distribution reshaping using ϵ-portion similarity. It is also crucial to notice that the standard KL divergence is defined when they have only non-zero entries; in our setup, this implies that all bins should be non-empty to ensure κ-KL similarity is well-defined. Here we omit details, but one may employ some heuristics: (1) Omit counting bin j where both $\mathcal{D}_{test}$ and $\mathcal{D}_{op}$ have no contribution to bin j. (2) When $\mathcal{D}_{test}$ contributes to bin j but not $\mathcal{D}_{op}$, return "undefined" or "∞" for the κ-KL similarity.

Finally, when κ-KL similarity is well-defined, provided that ϵ-portion-similarity holds, one can also derive a conservative κ value where the κ-KL-divergence-similarity measure is guaranteed to hold. It can be accomplished by considering a worst case where "every" bin in operation has the largest difference characterized by ϵ-portion-similarity (which is overly conservative, as the sum of all bin-ratios for operation will not be 1), followed by feeding that information to the definition of κ-KL-divergence similarity, in order to derive a conservative bounding κ value.

Note that for simplicity, we have prepared our formulation such that the distribution similarity is defined based on considering all neurons in layer l_A and having a unified binning function for all neurons. The constraint can be easily relaxed to allow distribution similarity to be considered only on a subset of neurons as well as neurons on different layers.

4 MILP Encoding for Distribution Reshaping

Provided that $\mathcal{D}_{op}$ and $\mathcal{D}_{test}$ are not similar in distribution, we are interested in finding a subset of $\mathcal{D}_{test}$, such that the subset has the similar distribution with $\mathcal{D}_{op}$. However, this is not an easy task, as demonstrated in the example in Fig. 2: When one only looks at the distribution in $i = 1$ and removes data point in_1 in $\mathcal{D}_{test}$ to create distribution similarity, it can create a negative impact on $i = 2$, where the reduction may not be desired.

When one finds such a subset, due to the distribution similarity one can estimate the performance. However, keeping the subset as large as possible is also desired. This leads to Definition 4, where we artificially introduce $\mathcal{D}_{can}$ to restrict the set of data points further as candidates to be removed. When $\mathcal{D}_{can}$ equals $\mathcal{D}_{test}$, any data point within $\mathcal{D}_{test}$ can be removed. As demonstrated in later paragraphs, in our MILP encoding scheme, the number of 0–1 integer variables introduced in the MILP equals the size of $\mathcal{D}_{can}$.

Definition 4 (Distribution Reshaping for ϵ-portion similarity via Test Set Reduction). *Provided that $\mathcal{D}_{op}$ and $\mathcal{D}_{test}$ are not ϵ-portion similar, given $\mathcal{D}_{can} \subseteq \mathcal{D}_{test}$, find $\mathcal{D}_{can}^{opt} \subseteq \mathcal{D}_{can}$ such that*

1. $\forall i \in \{1, \dots, d_l\}$, $\mathcal{D}_{op}$ *and* $\mathcal{D}_{test} \setminus \mathcal{D}_{can}^{opt}$ *are ϵ-portion similar.*
2. *The size of $\mathcal{D}_{can}^{opt}$ is minimum, among any other multiset $\mathcal{D}_{can}'$ that also ensures the first condition.*

If we take a data point in $\in \mathcal{D}_{can}$, pass it to the DNN and extracts $F^l(\text{in})$, apply the binning function on each computed neuron value $F_i^l(\text{in})$, this leads to a vector $v_{\text{in}} \stackrel{\text{def}}{:=} (b_N^{c,\Delta}(F_1^l(\text{in})), \dots, b_N^{c,\Delta}(F_{d_l}^l(\text{in}))) \in \{0, \dots, N\}^{d_l}$, where the value in each dimension $i \in \{1, \dots, d_l\}$ contains the associated binning information for the i-th output.

For every in $\in \mathcal{D}_{can}$, in our MILP encoding, create a 0–1 integer variable br_{in} that controls the decision of removing data point in from $\mathcal{D}_{can}$.

- If $br_{\text{in}} = 1$, then remove the data point in from $\mathcal{D}_{test}$.
- If $br_{\text{in}} = 0$, then keep the data point in.

For neuron i, recall that the number of elements originally in bin j equals $\text{ct}(j, B_i^{l_A}(F, \mathcal{D}_{test}))$. For data point in $\in \mathcal{D}_{can}$, if $F_i^{l_A}(\text{in})$ falls into bin j, then if we remove the data point, the size of remaining elements in bin j can be characterized as $\text{ct}(j, B_i^{l_A}(F, \mathcal{D}_{test})) - br_{\text{in}}$. Therefore, depending on the decision whether elements in $\mathcal{D}_{can}$ are removed or not, the number of elements for neuron i, bin j can be encoded as $\text{ct}(j, B_i^{l_A}(F, \mathcal{D}_{test})) - \sum_{\text{in} \in \mathcal{D}_{can} \text{ s.t. } b_N^{c,\Delta}(F_i^l(\text{in})) = j} br_{\text{in}}$.

Lemma 2 (MILP encoding). *The problem in Definition 4 can be reduced to the following MILP problem.*

$$minimize \sum_{in \in \mathcal{D}_{can}} br_{in} \ s.t.$$

$$\forall i \in \{1, \ldots, d_l\}, \forall j \in \{0, \ldots, N\} :$$

$$-\epsilon \leq \frac{ct(j, B_i^{l_A}(F, \mathcal{D}_{op}))}{|\mathcal{D}_{op}|} - \frac{ct(j, B_i^{l_A}(F, \mathcal{D}_{test})) - \sum_{in \in \mathcal{D}_{can} \ s.t. \ b_N^{c,i,\Delta}(F_i^l(in))=j} br_{in}}{|\mathcal{D}_{test}| - \sum_{in \in \mathcal{D}_{can}} br_{in}} \leq \epsilon \quad (8)$$

Proof. The encoding is straightforward, where the only difference with Eq. 3 is (1) the update of the denominator from $|\mathcal{D}_{test}|$ to $|\mathcal{D}_{test}| - \sum_{in \in \mathcal{D}_{can}} br_{in}$, reflecting the potential decrease in the data points, and (2) the update of the nominator by subtracting $\sum_{in \in \mathcal{D}_{can} \ s.t. \ b_N^{c,i,\Delta}(f_i^l(in))=j} br_{in}$, counting the potential decrease of the number of items in bin j. The remaining task is to ensure that the encoding does not lead to non-linear constraints. This holds, as $\frac{ct(j, B_i^{l_A}(F, \mathcal{D}_{op}))}{|\mathcal{D}_{op}|}$ is a constant, one can rewrite the inequality by multiplying $|\mathcal{D}_{test}| - \sum_{in \in \mathcal{D}_{can}} br_{in}$. □

Example 2. Consider $\mathcal{D}_{can} \overset{def}{:=} \langle in_1, in_2, in_3 \rangle$, where for each element in $\mathcal{D}_{can}$, its binning information is listed in Table 2. Then consider $i = 3$ and $j = 4$ in Eq. 8, the inequality part can be rewritten into Eq. 9, where $\frac{ct(4, B_3^{l_A}(F, \mathcal{D}_{op}))}{|\mathcal{D}_{op}|}$, $|\mathcal{D}_{test}|$, and $ct(4, B_3^{l_A}(F, \mathcal{D}_{test}))$ are constants that can be computed before the MILP encoding. As ϵ is also a constant, Eq. 9 can be rewritten into two linear constraints.

$$-\epsilon \leq \frac{ct(4, B_3^{l_A}(F, \mathcal{D}_{op}))}{|\mathcal{D}_{op}|} - \frac{ct(4, B_3^{l_A}(F, \mathcal{D}_{test})) - br_{in_1} - br_{in_3}}{|\mathcal{D}_{test}| - br_{in_1} - br_{in_2} - br_{in_3}} \leq \epsilon \quad (9)$$

Remark 1. Whenever distribution reshaping does not involve multiple neurons, finding a subset of $\mathcal{D}_{test}$ to ensure ϵ-portion similarity can be done efficiently (with a greedy algorithm), and therefore no MILP encoding required. Reconsider the example in Fig. 2 where the goal is only to perform reshaping on $i = 1$. One can simply remove in_1, as there is no side effect that should be considered.

5   Evaluation

We have implemented the concept and performed an initial feasibility study based on the MNIST dataset [10]. We use Pytorch [13] to train the DNN and use Google OR-Tools[2] to solve the generated MILP problem. For distribution reshaping, we take 20 neurons in close-to-output layers. To simulate the "covariate shift", we have intentionally created the testing dataset with significantly

---

[2] https://developers.google.com/optimization.

Table 2. An example for the MILP encoding

	$b_N^{c,\Delta}(F_1^{l_A}(\cdot))$	$b_N^{c,\Delta}(F_2^{l_A}(\cdot))$	$b_N^{c,\Delta}(F_3^{l_A}(\cdot))$
in_1	1	4	4
in_2	2	1	2
in_3	0	3	4

more examples in classes "7", "8" and "9" (with each around 20%), and left classes "1" to "5" have a small portion. The created operational dataset consists of 5300 image samples[3], where the portion of "7", "8" and "9" is significantly reduced, meaning that the assumption on the frequency for class distribution is incorrect. Recall that in our problem definition, one does not have access to the operational data and the associated ground truth labels. The experimental setting here allows us to estimate whether distribution reshaping on neurons (representing the feature space) positively correlates with the data distribution reflected by the associated label. For measuring similarity, we use the bin width $\Delta = 1$ and set ϵ to be 0.01. The set $\mathcal{D}_{can}$, i.e., elements that can be removed for distribution reshaping purposes, ranges from 7000 to 20000. This implies that in the corresponding MILP problem, we have a maximum of 20000 binary integer variables. The whole program and the MILP solver are operated on an Intel i5-9300H laptop equipped with 32GB RAM. Altogether the time required to find the smallest set to be removed for distribution reshaping is commonly below 15 minutes. Figure 3 shows the distribution for two neurons being considered.

Figure 4 presents our preliminary result, where in Fig. 4a, one can observe that although we only perform distribution reshaping on neurons reflecting the feature level, the reshaped test data is moving closer to the operational data when we consider the distribution reflected as the relative frequencies of each class, suggesting that the SPI estimation on the reshaped test dataset can be more precise. Figure 4b shows an aggregated result on all experiments being conducted, where the x coordinate characterizes the sum of the per-class ratio-difference between operational and reshaped test data, and the y coordinate characterizes the sum of the per-class ratio-difference between operational and the original test data. It also turned out that most of the points are within the top-left region, hinting that the reshaped test data demonstrates a positive correlation with the label distribution of the operational data.

6   Concluding Remarks

We investigated the problem of estimating the safety performance in the presence of covariate shift based on test data and (feature-level) neuron value distributions – but not on operational data, which often is unavailable in real-world situations.

---

[3] The set of 5300 images is a set of data that we intentionally manipulate to create covariance shift and treat it as data being collected in the field.

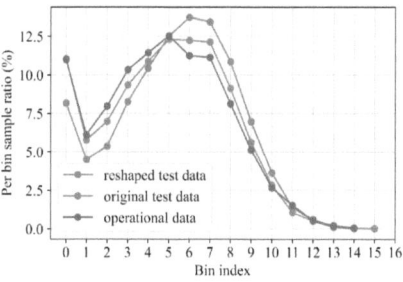 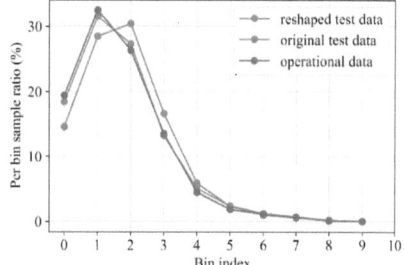

(a) Activation values binned for the 5th neuron

(b) Activation values binned for the 7th neuron

Fig. 3. Qualitative result of distribution reshaping simultaneously on multiple neurons

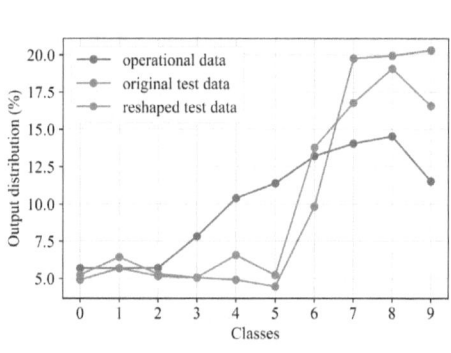 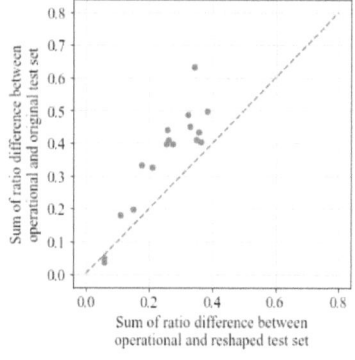

(a) Output distribution in one experiment

(b) Aggregated result

Fig. 4. Effect of distribution reshaping, observed on the output label distribution

Our main contribution is a MILP encoding for reshaping the test data to be similar to the (unknown) distribution of the operational data. This reshaped test data now serves as a proxy for evaluating the safety performance in the presence of covariate shift. With this approach, we may compute the distribution profile (as histograms) locally on the device of the DNN under investigation, thereby addressing possible privacy concerns. Initial experiments demonstrate the feasibility of this constraint-solving approach, but, clearly, more experience for more complex scenarios in real-world situations is needed. However, the maximum number of removable samples is restricted, as this number correlates with the number of 0–1 variables in the generated MILP problem. Constraint solving, in particular, needs to be accelerated considerably. Since the generated MILP encodings are highly-stylized, specialized variable branching heuristics or suitable polynomial-time approximation schemes may be developed. Finally, the problem of reshaping test data can be generalized to also adapt individual test data points to covariate shift based on their respective resilience bounds [2].

Acknowledgements. This work is supported by the StMWi Bayern as part of the project for the thematic development of the Fraunhofer IKS.

References

1. ANSI/UL 4600: Standard For Evaluation of Autonomous Products. Standard (2020)
2. Cheng, C.-H., Nührenberg, G., Ruess, H.: Maximum resilience of artificial neural networks. In: D'Souza, D., Narayan Kumar, K. (eds.) ATVA 2017. LNCS, vol. 10482, pp. 251–268. Springer, Cham (2017). https://doi.org/10.1007/978-3-319-68167-2_18
3. Fraade-Blanar, L.: Marjory S Blumenthal, James M Anderson, and Nidhi Kalra. Forging a framework, Measuring automated vehicle safety (2018)
4. Gao, S., Ver Steeg, G., Galstyan, A.: Efficient estimation of mutual information for strongly dependent variables. In: Artificial Intelligence and Statistics, pp. 277–286. PMLR (2015)
5. Gehr, T., et al.: Ai2: safety and robustness certification of neural networks with abstract interpretation. In: Proceedings of the 2018 IEEE Symposium on Security and Privacy (SP), pp. 3–18. IEEE (2018)
6. Gowal, S., et al.: Scalable verified training for provably robust image classification. In: Proceedings of the 2019 IEEE/CVF International Conference on Computer Vision (ICCV), pp. 4842–4851 (2019)
7. Koopman, P., Wagner, M.: Positive trust balance for self-driving car deployment. In: Casimiro, A., Ortmeier, F., Schoitsch, E., Bitsch, F., Ferreira, P. (eds.) SAFECOMP 2020. LNCS, vol. 12235, pp. 351–357. Springer, Cham (2020). https://doi.org/10.1007/978-3-030-55583-2_26
8. Kouw, W.M., Loog, M.: An introduction to domain adaptation and transfer learning. arXiv preprint arXiv:1812.11806 (2019)
9. Kraskov, A., Stögbauer, H., Grassberger, P.: Estimating mutual information. Phys. Rev. E **69**(6), 066138 (2004)
10. LeCun, Y.: The MNIST database of handwritten digits (1998). http://yann.lecun.com/exdb/mnist/
11. Lust, J., Condurache, A.P.: A survey on assessing the generalization envelope of deep neural networks: predictive uncertainty, out-of-distribution and adversarial samples. arXiv preprint arXiv:2008.09381 (2020)
12. McAllester, D., Stratos, K.: Formal limitations on the measurement of mutual information. In: International Conference on Artificial Intelligence and Statistics, pp. 875–884. PMLR (2020)
13. Paszke, A., et al.: Pytorch: an imperative style, high-performance deep learning library. In: Advances in Neural Information Processing Systems (NeurIPS), vol. 32 (2019)
14. Quinonero-Candela, J., Sugiyama, M., Schwaighofer, A., Lawrence, N.D.: Dataset Shift in Machine Learning. MIT Press (2008)
15. Ruff, L., et al.: A unifying review of deep and shallow anomaly detection. Proc. IEEE **109**(5), 756–795 (2021)
16. Vogel, R., Achab, M., Clémençon, S., Tillier, C.: Weighted empirical risk minimization: sample selection bias correction based on importance sampling. arXiv preprint arXiv:2002.05145 (2020)

Pierce: A Testing Tool for Neural Network Verification Solvers

Joseph Scott[1]([✉]) [iD], Guanting Pan[1]([✉]) [iD], Piyush Jha[1]([✉]) [iD],
Elias B. Khalil[2]([✉]) [iD], and Vijay Ganesh[1]([✉]) [iD]

[1] University of Waterloo, Waterloo, ON, Canada
{joseph.scott,g6pan,piyush.jha,vijay.ganesh}@uwaterloo.ca
[2] University of Toronto, Toronto, ON, Canada
khalil@mie.utoronto.ca

Abstract. We introduce `Pierce`, a versatile and extensible testing tool aimed at solvers for the neural network verification (NNV) problem. At its core, `Pierce` implements a fuzzing engine over the Open Neural Network Exchange (ONNX) – a standardized model format for deep learning and classical machine learning, and VNN-LIB – a specification standard over the input-output behavior of machine learning systems. `Pierce` supports the entirety of the VNN-LIB and most of ONNX v18. The API of `Pierce` is designed to enable users to create a variety of software testing tools, such as performance and mutation fuzzers, as well as delta debuggers, with relative ease. For example, `Pierce` provides a rich generator for computation graphs and specifications that allows users to easily specify a wide variety of configurations, as well as mutators that ensure that mutated computation graphs are well-formed.

Using `Pierce` we build a reinforcement learning (RL) driven relative performance fuzzer. Using this fuzzer, we expose performance issues in four state-of-the-art solvers, such as Marabou, ERAN, MIPVerify, and nnenum, observing up to a 13.3x times slowdown in cumulative `PAR-2` score in the target solvers relative to reference solvers. Further, we leverage `Pierce` to create a diverse benchmark suite with 10,000 competition-grade NNV instances for the community.

Keywords: AI Testing · Fuzzing · Neural Network Verification

1 Introduction

In recent years neural networks (NNs) have had a revolutionary impact on a variety of fields such as computer vision [13], natural language processing [32], and games [28], to name just a few. Concomitant with their widespread adoption in many settings, we are also witnessing a dramatic rise in security attacks on NNs, as well as robustness and safety issues associated with NNs such as local robustness [15].

To address the above-mentioned problems, the software engineering and verification communities have developed a variety of testing [20], analysis [30],

A. Reynolds and S. Tasiran (Eds.): VSTTE 2023, LNCS 14095, pp. 31–43, 2024.
https://doi.org/10.1007/978-3-031-66064-1_3

and neural network verification (NNV) tools such as Marabou [18], ERAN [29], MIPVerify [31], and nnenum [2]. While the field of NNV is still in its infancy, these NNV solvers are likely to have a huge positive impact on the robustness and security of NNs in the long run, just as SAT and SMT solvers have had on the field of software engineering and security [8, 9]. Part of the reason why SAT and SMT solvers are so impactful is that they have been subjected to a significant amount of testing, especially through the use of automated fuzzers [6, 26, 34].

Inspired by the success of debugging, testing, and analysis tools in the context of SAT/SMT solvers [4, 6, 14, 19, 21, 22, 26, 27, 33–35], we propose Pierce, a highly configurable testing tool for NNV solvers. Developers of NNV solvers can use Pierce to quickly create mutation and performance fuzzers, as well as delta debuggers. We use Pierce to create a performance fuzzer that can be used out-of-the-box by NNV solver developers to find performance weaknesses in their solver relative to a set of reference solvers.

Recently, it has been shown that reinforcement learning (RL) techniques can be used to develop powerful fuzzing tools that naturally take advantage of the feedback loop between the fuzzer (agent) and the testing oracle with the programs-under-test (environment) [7]. This idea is particularly relevant in the case of performance fuzzing (say in the context of solvers), where relative performance between a target and reference solver can be a powerful signal in guiding an agent to effectively modify an instance such that the relative performance difference between target and reference solvers is maximized [26, 27, 37]. To demonstrate Pierce's versatility, we provide a case study implementing a relative performance fuzzer. With Pierce, we fuzz Marabou, ERAN, MIPVerify, and nnenum, for relative performance issues and observe up to a 13.3x times slowdown between a target and a set of reference solvers.

Contributions

1. **The Pierce Tool.** We present Pierce tool for developing testing tools for Neural Network Verification (NNV) solvers (see Sect. 3 and architecture diagram in Fig. 2). Pierce provides its users with two key capabilities. First, it has a computation graph generator that can generate graphs that correspond to random graphs, decision trees, and NNs (including those that are VNN-LIB compliant), whose shape (e.g., number of inputs and outputs, width, height, number of parameters, etc.) can be specified by the user using a configuration file. Second, Pierce has a mutator (i.e., a set of well-defined mutation operators) that mutates computation graphs in a well-formed manner. These and other capabilities make Pierce a highly configurable, extensible, and easy-to-use tool (Sect. 3.2) with many possible use cases (Sect. 3.3). For example, a user of Pierce can write a relatively straightforward script to configure Pierce into a debugging or performance fuzzer for NNV solvers.

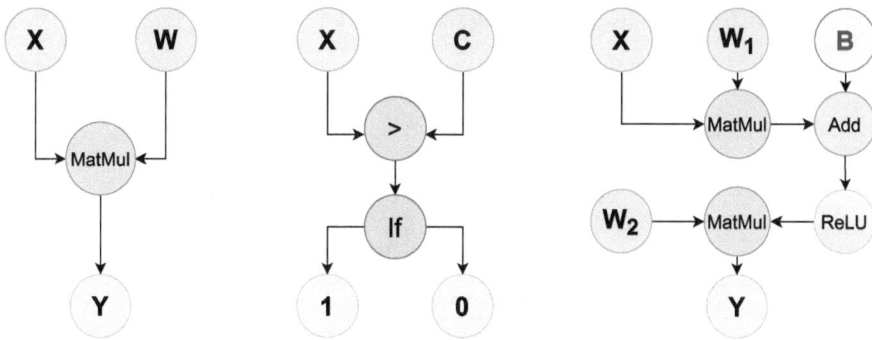

Fig. 1. Three example computation graphs, each of which outlines a common ML algorithm. From left to right: linear regression, a depth one decision tree, a deep neural network with a single hidden layer, ReLU activation, and linear output activation. The *MatMul* stands for Matrix Multiplication.

2. **Reinforcement Learning driven Performance Fuzzing of Neural Network Verifiers.** We configure `Pierce` into a performance fuzzer that is aimed at finding small instances that expose performance issues in a target solver relative to a set of reference solvers (Sect. 4). For example, we found instances that resulted in significant empirical slowdowns for four state-of-the-art neural network verification solvers, namely ERAN, Marabou, MIPVerify, and nnenum [2,18,29,31]. This is done via a reinforcement learning fuzzing loop based on recent work [27]. The instances our fuzzer generated show a slowdown of 13.3x of target solver (e.g., ERAN) relative to a set of reference solvers (e.g., Marabou, MIPVerify, and nnenum).

3. **A Repository of Benchmarks.** We provide a rich repository of benchmark suite of over 10,000 competition-grade instances, unit, and regression tests in ONNX format produced using `Pierce` (Sect. 3.3). The benchmarks are broad, covering a variety of problem classes and configurations.

2 Preliminaries

Computation Graphs. Informally, a computation graph C is an abstract syntax-tree-like data structure that embeds the control flow of arbitrary machine learning programs. A node, $n \in C$, is made of an operator ϕ, a set of inputs X, and a set of outputs Y. While computation graphs are often exclusively considered in the context of deep learning, their expressibility is much richer. For example, consider Fig. 1 showing three example computation graphs, linear regression, a depth one decision tree, and a deep neural network with a single hidden layer, ReLU activation, and linear output activation.

The Open Neural Network Exchange (ONNX). ONNX is a research and industrial initiative to standardize machine learning models [12]. In the latest

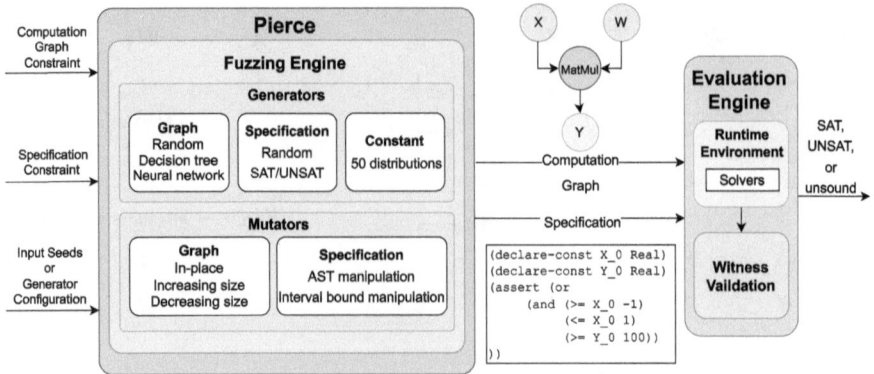

Fig. 2. Architecture Diagram of `Pierce` (See Sect. 3). `Pierce` is comprised of a fuzzing engine that enables the generation and mutation of VNN-LIB benchmarks.

ONNX V18, the syntax and semantics of computation graphs are outlined over 187 operations. ONNX is widely supported across major deep learning platforms, such as: TensorFlow [1], PyTorch [23], and Keras [11]. Furthermore, it is widely supported across major machine learning APIs, such as: scikit-learn [24] and XGBoost [10].

The VNN-LIB Initiative. The VNN-LIB is an international initiative with the aim is to support researchers in verifying neural networks [16]. As discussed in Sect. 1, a verification query requires two parts, a computation graph C and a specification ψ. For C, VNN-LIB defines syntax and semantics leveraging a subset of 17 ONNX operations, with the 2021 competition benchmarks leveraging 15 operators.

3 `Pierce`: A Testing Tool for Machine Learning Verification Tools

In this section, we describe `Pierce`, a testing tool for ML verification (see architecture diagram in Fig. 2).

3.1 Architecture Overview

See Fig. 2 for the architecture of `Pierce`. In the context of ML verification, the input (or problem *instance*) to an ML verification system is a computation graph C and a specification ψ over the input-output behavior of C, and the output SAT (VIOLATED) or UNSAT (SAFE). The primary objective of the fuzzing engine is two-fold: generate novel instances and mutate instances, stochastically.

Generation of Computation Graphs. The generator API of `Pierce` takes as input a configuration file that includes all the parameters (approx. 550, e.g., number of parameters, depth, operator weights, etc.) for creating novel graphs, and outputs an appropriate computation graph in the ONNX format. In a computation graph, all types within the graph are tensors (i.e., a generalization of a matrix) over a primitive data type (e.g., a tensor of float32). The bulk of the logic within `Pierce`'s generator is to ensure all type, dimensionality, arity, and coarity[1] constraints are satisfied. The dimensionalities of all tensors are selected from a randomly populated set of permissible dimensions (shapes). To populate the computation graph, the generator implements a breadth-first scheme, with each visit sampling the set of operators. Cycles in G are disabled by default and not considered in this paper. In scenarios where graph widths are significantly disproportional to the output, the generator imposes coarity constraints on the operation selection. Furthermore, in scenarios where dimensions cannot be matched precisely, appropriate ones are allocated. There are several size parameters in the generation process to enable the generation of graphs of all sorts of sizes (e.g., tens to billions of parameters).

The generation process supports four problem classes. First, *randomized graphs*: this is the most random and expressive problem class, representative of arbitrary machine learning programs. Second, `Pierce` can generate computation graphs resembling *decision trees*, computation graphs that contain several nested conditionals over features and constants. Third, `Pierce` can generate computation graphs resembling *random neural architectures*. This is done internally by sampling a subgraph rather than operators in the breadth-first search, where the subgraph is a composition of operators resembling a common neural layer. We leverage 20 subgraphs that denote familiar layers from `torch.nn` [23]. Finally, `Pierce` can generate *VNN-LIB graphs*, which is a subset of the previous class, such that all operators within layers are consistent with the VNN-LIB standard.

Generation of Specifications. The typical specification for a given computation graph is a set of constraints that bound the values of the input and outputs of a given computation graph. That is, a specification is either a static ϵ_x, ϵ_y pair or a component-wise $\epsilon_{ix}, \epsilon_{iy}$, (e.g., $x \in [x'_i - \epsilon_{ix}, x'_i + \epsilon_{ix}], y \in [y'_i - \epsilon_{iy}, y'_i + \epsilon_{iy}]$). The point within the domain and codomain vector space that forms the bounding is denoted by x', y', respectively. x' is always chosen randomly, while y', ϵ, ϵ' depends on the problem class. Further assertions are added randomly. These assertions can either be linear constraints – disjunctions, conjunctions, and linear integer real arithmetic, or nonlinear. We exclusively consider linear constraints for the remainder of the paper.

`Pierce` can generate a variety of classes of specification constraints, ranging from random specifications to specifications with known results. For example,

---

[1] arity of output.

`Pierce` can generate instances where we known that it is SAT (i.e., the specification is guaranteed to be violated). This is done by computing $y' = C(x')$ for a given computation graph C and randomly-generated input x', and generating additional constraint set A on the output of C that guarantee y' is within the bounds defined by A. Furthermore, `Pierce` can generate specifications that are UNSAT with high probability. This is done by first computing $y'' = C(x')$ for a given graph C and randomly generated input x', and then ensuring that the bounds asserted by the constraint set A on the output y'' and for a perturbation Δ with a large budget $y' = y'' + \Delta$. While the result isn't guaranteed to be UNSAT, we observe this to be highly probable for significantly large Δ and ϵ_i.

Mutating Computation Graphs and Specifications. `Pierce` has a mutator (i.e., a set of mutation operators) that ensures that a computation graph G is modified in a well-formed manner. A single mutation implements a minimal structural change. Similar to generation, the bulk of the logic is devoted to ensuring that all types, dimensionalities, arity, and coarity constraints are satisfied. For computation graph mutations, it can be done either in-place (i.e., the size of the graph remains the same) or by increasing/decreasing the size of the graph.

In-place mutations are conceptually similar to AST manipulation schemes in BanditFuzz [27]. If the mutation is applied to a computation graph C, then a node is selected, and a node of the appropriate return sort is used in an in-place swap. With incompatible coarities, subgraphs are appropriately dropped or regenerated. Increasing mutations allow for increases in dimensionality (this changes both C, ψ), insertion of a new node in C, or insertion of a new node in an asserting AST in ψ. Decreasing mutations are analogous.

A desirable property of a mutational fuzzer is satisfiability preservation, i.e., if a computation graph C is SAT (resp. UNSAT), then it remains SAT (resp. UNSAT) after mutation. Such a feature makes the fuzzer very valuable to solver developers. To see this consider the following scenario: suppose a computation graph (along with its specification) C which is known to be SAT is mutated in a satisfiability-preserving manner to C', and a solver S outputs UNSAT on C' then we know that solver S has a bug in it. This idea has been explored extensively in SMT [35]. `Pierce` includes two simple mutation procedures to support this feature. Namely, on SAT benchmarks, `Pierce` has a mutation procedure that increases the bound on the input/output of the instance and, analogously for UNSAT, decreases it.

Constant Generation. `Pierce` supports a diverse set of seven probability distributions to generate constants. For example, `Pierce` leverages: Normal, Uniform, geometric, Beta, Gamma, Zipf, and Rayleigh. `Pierce` uses several values for the parameters of the probability distribution to compute the final set. When generating a constant tensor, the set of distributions is sampled to populate it.

Evaluation Engine. We include an evaluation engine for additional utility. The evaluation engine collects system information (e.g., wall-clock times, memory, etc.) and comes with a base solver class and example-derived classes over select

VNN-LIB solvers for a quick extension. `Pierce` comes with witness validation to determine if the solver soundly determined satisfiability.

Implementation Details. `Pierce` is implemented in Python version 3.8, and uses both `onnx` and `onnxruntime` to implement all components in the fuzzing engine. `Pierce` uses `numpy` [17] for its random constant generation and all other random processes. The execution engine leverages `benchexec` [5].

3.2   Command Line Interfaces

`Pierce` can be invoked in three different modes depending on the CLI option - fuzz (generate a novel instance), mut (mutate a pre-existing instance), or eval (evaluate an instance on a solver).

Fuzzing. In the fuzzing mode, `Pierce` expects an argument denoting the graph problem class {rand, tree, dnn, vnnlib} for generating random computation graphs, decision tree-like graphs, neural network-like graphs, and VNN-LIB compliant graphs, respectively. Additionally, the specification problem class {rand, sat, punsat} also needs to be specified.

Mutating. In the mutating mode, `Pierce` expects an argument denoting mutation mode {graph, spec, graph-up, graph-down, preserve-sat, preserve-unsat} and a specified graph C with specification ψ for an input seed.

Evaluating. In the evaluation mode, a user specifies an instance and a solver to be evaluated. `Pierce` outputs a summary of computational resources used and the result of the solver.

Configuration. Both fuzzing and mutation processes are highly stochastic. However, significant effort has been made to ensure the user had a significant ability to adjust this process. We provide a detailed YAML file with over 500 adjustable hyperparameters[2]. These parameters control weighted probabilities of operators, random number generators, and the generation and mutation process of the fuzzing engine.

3.3   Potential Use Cases

`Pierce` is engineered and designed so it can be leveraged by ML verification developers to help improve the efficiency and efficacy of their tools. We next outline some example usage.

Benchmark Generation and Testing. The generator of `Pierce`'s fuzzing system allows for benchmarks of extreme varieties and problem classes. A developer can leverage `Pierce` to create instances ranging from unit tests, regression tests, to competition difficulty instances. We release a repository of 10,000 benchmarks to the community produced by `Pierce`. The first 4,950 instances are small unit tests. These tests are broken down to test the functionality of all 187 operations of the ONNX standard. The next 4,950 instances are medium-sized instances resembling regression tests. These benchmarks are evenly distributed into their

---

[2] Note that these hyperparameters have reasonable default values that can make it operate in a click-of-a-button.

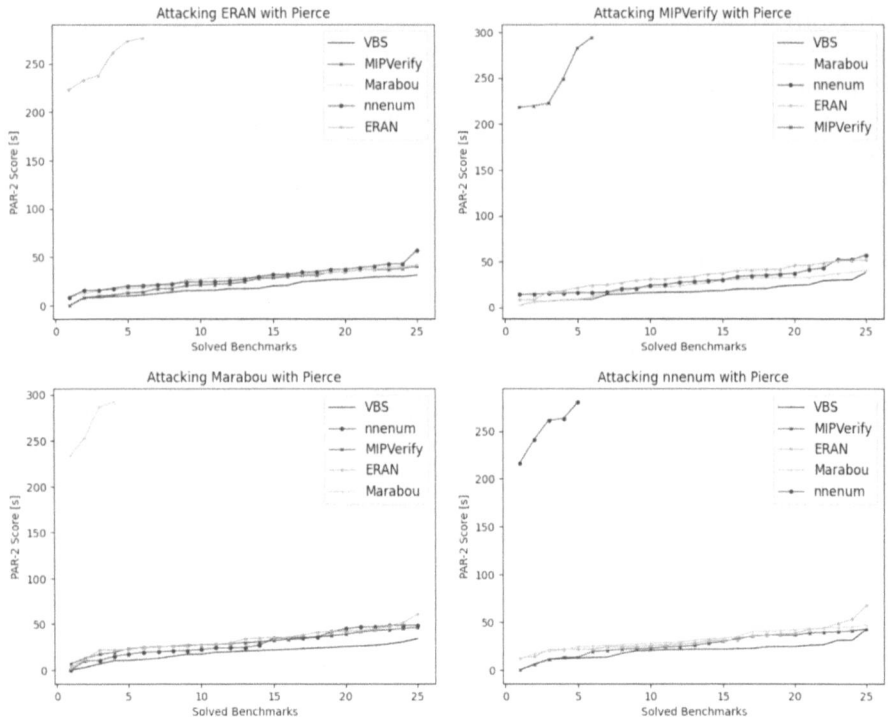

Fig. 3. Main experimental cactus plots demonstrating `Pierce`'s ability to reveal relative performance slowdowns (Sect. 4). A cactus plot is a visualization of a solver's performance on a benchmark suite the X-axis represents the number of benchmarks solved (higher is better) and the Y-axis is the benchmark wise `PAR-2` (lower is better).

respective problem classes. The final 100 are competition-grade benchmarks that are compliant with VNN-LIB. We intend to submit these to future competitions.

Fuzzing. `Pierce` has an extensive and highly configurable fuzzing engine that can be leveraged to build several fuzzers for various objectives.

Delta Debugging. A delta-debugger is a tool to decrease the size of an error-revealing instance I such that I is minimal in size and the erroneous behavior of the program-under-test is preserved. `Pierce` has an extensive and highly configurable mutational engine that can be leveraged to build a delta debugger.

4   Case Study: Reinforcement Learning Guided Performance Fuzzing with `Pierce`

In this section, we present an empirical case study of `Pierce`. Specifically, we use `Pierce`'s fuzzing utility and leverage it to find relative performance slowdowns across NNV solvers by leveraging an adaption of the BanditFuzz algorithm [26].

Table 1. Table of sums of PAR-2 across all experiments from the empirical evaluation (Sect. 4). The PAR-2 score of a solver on a benchmark is the wall-clock runtime if successful, otherwise twice the wall-clock runtime (lower is better). VBS denotes the virtual best solver. We observe that Pierce is able to discover instances with relative slowdowns across all considered solvers.

Targeting MIPVerify		Targeting nnenum	
Solver	PAR-2	Solver	PAR-2
VBS	453.5	VBS	507.2
Marabou	597.0	MIPVerify	659.0
nnenum	738.7	ERAN	786.1
ERAN	840.2	Marabou	802.0
MIPVerify	10079.8	nnenum	10057.6
Targeting ERAN		Targeting Marabou	
Solver	PAR-2	Solver	PAR-2
VBS	453.5	VBS	507.2
MIPVerify	605.8	nnenum	720.4
Marabou	688.3	MIPVerify	755.2
nnenum	725.5	ERAN	815.7
ERAN	10351.9	Marabou	10899.4

4.1 Experimental Setup

Relative Performance Fuzzing. Let T be a set of solvers to be targeted, and let R be a set of reference solvers. Let ϕ be an empirical performance margin function. The relative performance fuzzing problem seeks to solve

$$\max_{I \in L} \phi(T, R, I)$$

for a set of target solvers T, reference solvers R, and input I in the language L over solvers in T, R. In this paper, we exclusively consider the following performance margin function

$$\phi(T, R, I) = \min_{t \in T}(\text{PAR-2}(t, I)) - \max_{r \in R}(\text{PAR-2}(r, I))$$

Bandit Formulation. For full context on the use of reinforcement learning and multi-armed bandits (MAB) in the context of performance fuzzing we refer the reader to Scott et al. [27]. In this context, for a set of agents $\mathcal{A}$, each agent $A \in \mathcal{A}$, must have a defined action set to sample from and a global reward signal $\mathcal{R}$ across $\mathcal{A}$. For $\mathcal{R}$, we use a binary signal of whether or not the resultant benchmark produced an increase in the above-defined performance margin function. We include 5 agents in $\mathcal{A}$, controlling generator parameters of depth, width, dimensionality, and input/output sizes. We use Thompson Sampling as our base MAB algorithm [25].

Fuzzing Formulation. We consider four state-of-the-art solvers for VNN-LIB, namely, ERAN [29], Marabou [18], MIPVerify [31], and nnenum [2]. We run four fuzzing experiments, targeting each solver while using the remainder as reference solvers, and conducting each experiment 25 times to produce 25 benchmarks exposing slowdowns in each solver. Each experiment was run for 48 h. We configure `Pierce` to generate "small" with final benchmarks ranging from 10,000 to 50,000 parameters (i.e., 100–400 neurons).

Computational Environment. All experiments were performed on the Compute Canada computing service [3], a CentOS V7 cluster of Intel Xeon Processor E5-2683 running at 2.10 GHz with 8 GB of memory. Wall-clock runtimes are rounded to the nearest second, with a wall-clock timeout of 300 s. Solvers were configured to run sequentially. We observe `Pierce` to consistently find relative performance slowdowns.

4.2   Evaluation and Analysis of Results

The cactus plot of the evaluation is presented in Fig. 3. Table 1 presents the `PAR-2` all experiments. The `PAR-2` score of a solver on a benchmark is the wall-clock runtime if successful. Otherwise, twice the wall-clock runtime (lower is better). We see across all four fuzzing experiments, the target solver (in pink, last line of each legend) has a significant performance drop-off compared to the reference solvers. We include a comparison with the Virtual Best Solver (VBS). The VBS is an instance-wise minimum of runtimes which makes it representative of the best solver from a given set.

5   Related Work

To the best of our knowledge, we are not aware of previous work on fuzzing tools for ONNX and VNN-LIB. In other domains, such as SMT, there are analysis tools that motivated us to develop `Pierce`, such as StringFuzz [6], ddsmt [19,19,22], and BanditFuzz [26,27]. BanditFuzz is a fuzzing algorithm that applies Reinforcement Learning (RL) to generate inputs for Floating-Point (FP) and String SMT solvers. The RL objective of BanditFuzz is to maximize the performance margin between target and reference solvers. Counterexample-Guided Fuzzing for Neural Networks Verification is designed to discover neural network verification tools' mistakes [36]. To get more counterexamples in a sample set with a limited size and improve the performance in uncovering errors, the scope of the sample space is reduced continuously based on the generated counterexamples.

6   Conclusions

In this chapter, we presented Pierce, a flexible testing system that can be used to construct a variety of fuzzers and delta debuggers to test NNV solvers, as well as for other machine learning settings such as decision trees. To showcase the versatility and utility of Pierce, we implemented a relative performance fuzzer using it that in turn exposed relative performance slowdown in four state-of-the-art NNV solvers, namely, Marabou, ERAN, MIPVerify, and nnenum. We observed up to a substantial slowdown in target solvers relative to reference ones. Further, using Pierce we created 10,000 diverse benchmarks spanning unit tests, regression tests, and competition grade benchmarks.

References

1. Abadi, M., et al.: TensorFlow: large-scale machine learning on heterogeneous distributed systems. CoRR abs/1603.04467 (2016). http://arxiv.org/abs/1603.04467
2. Bak, S.: nnenum: verification of ReLU neural networks with optimized abstraction refinement. In: Dutle, A., Moscato, M.M., Titolo, L., Muñoz, C.A., Perez, I. (eds.) NFM 2021. LNCS, vol. 12673, pp. 19–36. Springer, Cham (2021). https://doi.org/10.1007/978-3-030-76384-8_2
3. Baldwin, S.: Compute Canada: advancing computational research. J. Phys: Conf. Ser. **341**, 012001 (2012)
4. Balyo, T., Heule, M., Jarvisalo, M.: SAT competition 2016: recent developments. In: Proceedings of the AAAI Conference on Artificial Intelligence, vol. 31 (2017)
5. Beyer, D., Löwe, S., Wendler, P.: Reliable benchmarking: requirements and solutions. Int. J. Softw. Tools Technol. Transf. **21**(1), 1–29 (2019). https://doi.org/10.1007/s10009-017-0469-y
6. Blotsky, D., Mora, F., Berzish, M., Zheng, Y., Kabir, I., Ganesh, V.: StringFuzz: a fuzzer for string solvers. In: Chockler, H., Weissenbacher, G. (eds.) CAV 2018, Part II. LNCS, vol. 10982, pp. 45–51. Springer, Cham (2018). https://doi.org/10.1007/978-3-319-96142-2_6
7. Böttinger, K., Godefroid, P., Singh, R.: Deep reinforcement fuzzing. In: 2018 IEEE Security and Privacy Workshops, SP Workshops 2018, San Francisco, CA, USA, 24 May 2018, pp. 116–122. IEEE Computer Society (2018). https://doi.org/10.1109/SPW.2018.00026
8. Cadar, C., Dunbar, D., Engler, D.R.: KLEE: unassisted and automatic generation of high-coverage tests for complex systems programs. In: Draves, R., van Renesse, R. (eds.) Proceedings of the 8th USENIX Symposium on Operating Systems Design and Implementation, OSDI 2008, 8–10 December 2008, San Diego, California, USA, pp. 209–224. USENIX Association (2008). http://www.usenix.org/events/osdi08/tech/full_papers/cadar/cadar.pdf
9. Cadar, C., Ganesh, V., Pawlowski, P.M., Dill, D.L., Engler, D.R.: EXE: automatically generating inputs of death. ACM Trans. Inf. Syst. Secur. **12**(2), 10:1–10:38 (2008). https://doi.org/10.1145/1455518.1455522
10. Chen, T., Guestrin, C.: XGBoost: a scalable tree boosting system. In: Krishnapuram, B., Shah, M., Smola, A.J., Aggarwal, C.C., Shen, D., Rastogi, R. (eds.) Proceedings of the 22nd ACM SIGKDD International Conference on Knowledge Discovery and Data Mining, San Francisco, CA, USA, 13–17 August 2016, pp. 785–794. ACM (2016). https://doi.org/10.1145/2939672.2939785
11. Chollet, F., et al.: Keras (2015). https://keras.io
12. ONNX Runtime developers: ONNX runtime (2021). https://onnxruntime.ai/, version: x.y.z

13. Dosovitskiy, A., et al.: An image is worth 16x16 words: transformers for image recognition at scale. In: 9th International Conference on Learning Representations, ICLR 2021, Virtual Event, Austria, 3–7 May 2021. OpenReview.net (2021). https://openreview.net/forum?id=YicbFdNTTy

14. Froleyks, N., Heule, M., Iser, M., Järvisalo, M., Suda, M.: Sat competition 2020. Artif. Intell. **301**, 103572 (2021). https://doi.org/10.1016/j.artint.2021.103572

15. Goodfellow, I.J., Shlens, J., Szegedy, C.: Explaining and harnessing adversarial examples. In: Bengio, Y., LeCun, Y. (eds.) 3rd International Conference on Learning Representations, ICLR 2015, San Diego, CA, USA, 7–9 May 2015, Conference Track Proceedings (2015). http://arxiv.org/abs/1412.6572

16. Guidotti, D., Demarchi, S., Tacchella, A., Pulina, L.: The Verification of Neural Networks Library (VNN-LIB) (2019). www.vnnlib.org

17. Harris, C.R., et al.: Array programming with NumPy. nature **585**(7825), 357–362 (2020). https://doi.org/10.1038/s41586-020-2649-2

18. Katz, G., et al.: The Marabou framework for verification and analysis of deep neural networks. In: Dillig, I., Tasiran, S. (eds.) CAV 2019, Part I. LNCS, vol. 11561, pp. 443–452. Springer, Cham (2019). https://doi.org/10.1007/978-3-030-25540-4_26

19. Kremer, G., Niemetz, A., Preiner, M.: ddSMT 2.0: better delta debugging for the SMT-LIBv2 language and friends. In: Silva, A., Leino, K.R.M. (eds.) CAV 2021, Part II. LNCS, vol. 12760, pp. 231–242. Springer, Cham (2021). https://doi.org/10.1007/978-3-030-81688-9_11

20. Nagisetty, V.: Domain Knowledge Guided Testing and Training of Neural Networks. Master's thesis, University of Waterloo (2021). http://hdl.handle.net/10012/17272

21. Newsham, Z., Ganesh, V., Fischmeister, S., Audemard, G., Simon, L.: Impact of community structure on sat solver performance. In: Sinz, C., Egly, U. (eds.) SAT 2014. LNCS, vol. 8561, pp. 252–268. Springer, Cham (2014). https://doi.org/10.1007/978-3-319-09284-3_20

22. Niemetz, A., Biere, A.: ddSMT: a delta debugger for the SMT-LIB v2 format. In: Proceedings of the 11th International Workshop on Satisfiability Modulo Theories, SMT 2013, affiliated with the 16th International Conference on Theory and Applications of Satisfiability Testing, SAT 2013, Helsinki, Finland, 8–9 July 2013, pp. 36–45 (2013)

23. Paszke, A., et al.: PyTorch: an imperative style, high-performance deep learning library. In: Wallach, H.M., Larochelle, H., Beygelzimer, A., d'Alché-Buc, F., Fox, E.B., Garnett, R. (eds.) Advances in Neural Information Processing Systems 32: Annual Conference on Neural Information Processing Systems 2019, NeurIPS 2019, 8–14 December 2019, Vancouver, BC, Canada, pp. 8024–8035 (2019). https://proceedings.neurips.cc/paper/2019/hash/bdbca288fee7f92f2bfa9f7012727740-Abstract.html

24. Pedregosa, F., et al.: Scikit-learn: machine learning in Python. J. Mach. Learn. Res. **12**, 2825–2830 (2011). http://dl.acm.org/citation.cfm?id=2078195

25. Russo, D., Roy, B.V., Kazerouni, A., Osband, I., Wen, Z.: A tutorial on Thompson sampling. Found. Trends Mach. Learn. **11**(1), 1–96 (2018). https://doi.org/10.1561/2200000070

26. Scott, J., Mora, F., Ganesh, V.: BanditFuzz: a reinforcement-learning based performance fuzzer for SMT solvers. In: Christakis, M., Polikarpova, N., Duggirala, P.S., Schrammel, P. (eds.) NSV/VSTTE -2020. LNCS, vol. 12549, pp. 68–86. Springer, Cham (2020). https://doi.org/10.1007/978-3-030-63618-0_5

27. Scott, J., Sudula, T., Rehman, H., Mora, F., Ganesh, V.: BanditFuzz: fuzzing SMT solvers with multi-agent reinforcement learning. In: Huisman, M., Păsăreanu, C., Zhan, N. (eds.) FM 2021. LNCS, vol. 13047, pp. 103–121. Springer, Cham (2021). https://doi.org/10.1007/978-3-030-90870-6_6

28. Silver, D., et al.: Mastering chess and shogi by self-play with a general reinforcement learning algorithm. CoRR abs/1712.01815 (2017). http://arxiv.org/abs/1712.01815

29. Singh, G., et al.: ETH robustness analyzer for neural networks (ERAN) (2020). https://github.com/eth-sri/eran

30. Sotoudeh, M., Thakur, A.V.: SyReNN: a tool for analyzing deep neural networks. In: TACAS 2021, Part II. LNCS, vol. 12652, pp. 281–302. Springer, Cham (2021). https://doi.org/10.1007/978-3-030-72013-1_15

31. Tjeng, V., Tedrake, R.: Verifying neural networks with mixed integer programming. CoRR abs/1711.07356 (2017). http://arxiv.org/abs/1711.07356

32. Vaswani, A., et al.: Attention is all you need. In: Guyon, I., et al. (eds.) Advances in Neural Information Processing Systems 30: Annual Conference on Neural Information Processing Systems 2017, 4–9 December 2017, Long Beach, CA, USA, pp. 5998–6008 (2017). https://proceedings.neurips.cc/paper/2017/hash/3f5ee243547dee91fbd053c1c4a845aa-Abstract.html

33. Weber, T., Conchon, S., Déharbe, D., Heizmann, M., Niemetz, A., Reger, G.: The SMT competition 2015–2018. J. Satisf. Boolean Model. Comput. **11**(1), 221–259 (2019). https://doi.org/10.3233/SAT190123

34. Winterer, D., Zhang, C., Su, Z.: On the unusual effectiveness of type-aware operator mutations for testing SMT solvers. Proc. ACM Program. Lang. **4**(OOPSLA), 193:1–193:25 (2020). https://doi.org/10.1145/3428261

35. Winterer, D., Zhang, C., Su, Z.: Validating SMT solvers via semantic fusion. In: Donaldson, A.F., Torlak, E. (eds.) Proceedings of the 41st ACM SIGPLAN International Conference on Programming Language Design and Implementation, PLDI 2020, London, UK, 15–20 June 2020, pp. 718–730. ACM (2020). https://doi.org/10.1145/3385412.3385985

36. Yi, G., Wang, X., Wang, Y.: An empirical study of counterexample-guided fuzzing for neural networks verification. In: 7th International Conference on Dependable Systems and their Applications, DSA 2020, Xi'an, China, 28–29 November 2020, pp. 108–113. IEEE (2020). https://doi.org/10.1109/DSA51864.2020.00022

37. Zhang, Y., et al.: Demystifying performance regressions in string solvers. IEEE Trans. Softw. Eng. (2022). https://doi.org/10.1109/TSE.2022.3168373

Specifying and Verifying a Real-World Packet Error-Correction System

Joshua M. Cohen$^{(\boxtimes)}$ and Andrew W. Appel

Princeton University, Princeton, NJ 08544, USA
jmc16@princeton.edu

Abstract. Automated and semi-automated formal methods have been widely employed to verify properties of network models and *per-packet* network functions, which operate on single packets in the middle of a network (firewall, NAT, etc.). But these methods do not extend to *end-to-end* network functions, those whose specification relates a stream of packets sent at one endpoint of the network with a stream received at the other end. Among other complications, such specifications must account for the network's behavior, including packet reordering, duplication, delay, and loss. We develop a methodology for formally specifying and verifying such code, demonstrating our techniques on a real-world packet error-correction system that encounters all of these challenges and whose specification had been highly unclear. We prove a close model of this system correct in the Coq proof assistant; along the way, we formalize more general networking constructs including IP/UDP packets, a metric for packet reordering, and sequence number comparison. Finally, through our specification, we develop an improved version of the error-correction system, giving a more predictable, provably correct program that recovers more packets. We show that formal specification and verification can be powerful tools to clarify assumptions, improve code quality, and find and fix bugs in complex, real-world systems.

1 Introduction

Formal verification has been widely applied to networks and network components, whose correctness is critical for higher-level internet applications. Broadly, these efforts take one of two forms: verifying properties of entire networks (reachability, routing protocol convergence, etc.) by using automated solvers on a simple model of the network (e.g. a graph) or verifying network function implementations that operate per-packet and which are often implemented at the intermediate nodes of a network (NAT, firewall, etc.). Neither of these methods extends to *end-to-end* network functions: those run at the end hosts and whose specification cannot be expressed solely as a function of the input packet but must relate multiple packets in the stream. These include critical transport-layer functions for reliable delivery including packet reordering, congestion control, flow control, error correction, and packet retransmission mechanisms.

© The Author(s), under exclusive license to Springer Nature Switzerland AG 2024
A. Reynolds and S. Tasiran (Eds.): VSTTE 2023, LNCS 14095, pp. 44–63, 2024.
https://doi.org/10.1007/978-3-031-66064-1_4

Proving the correctness of per-packet functions generally involves reasoning about which header fields in a packet must change (based on the packet and stored data, e.g. a map of internal/external IPs for a NAT) and proving some related higher-level properties (e.g. a firewall blocks packets from a certain IP range). But end-to-end functions require a completely different approach, as they have several distinctive challenges. First, though executed packet-by-packet, their behavior (and thus, a specification) depends on the often-complex interactions between the entire stream of packets sent and received, as well as state at both ends. Second, such implementations typically use timeout mechanisms and may depend on additional external state such as the system time; their behavior depends not only on the packet inputs but on the ability of the network to drop, delay, reorder, and duplicate packets. Finally, the intended guarantees provided by such a system may be unclear; for instance, the system may be permitted to drop packets (say, if it has not seen a missing packet for a long time) or it could assume properties about the underlying network which may or may not hold.

In this paper, we investigate how formal specification and verification can be used to effectively reason about these types of real-world end-to-end systems. We use as an extended case study an existing, real-world packet error-correction system written in C; we determine a specification for it and verify a close model against this spec in the Coq proof assistant. The core error-correction algorithm and its C implementation were verified by Cohen *et al.* [12]; here we reason about the larger system to group, store, send, and receive packets at the end hosts. The core algorithm's verification was complex – requiring reasoning about sophisticated mathematics and low-level C programming conditions – but its specification was not, arising from well-known mathematical properties of the underlying Reed-Solomon code. In contrast, for packet reordering, duplicating, and timeouts, formulating a specification is difficult, both because of the end-to-end challenges discussed above and because this implementation violates any reasonable specification. We detail our process and demonstrate how to reason about code whose specification is unknown, dependent on external conditions, and reliant on invariants maintained through different executions, and we show that even the act of specifying a "dusty deck" program can clarify assumptions, find bugs, and lead to cleaner, more performant, and more predictable code. Our contributions are as follows:

1. We present a methodology for formally specifying real-world, end-to-end network functions, especially transport-layer programs for reliable delivery.
2. We apply these techniques to specify and verify in the Coq proof assistant a real-world error-correction system, the first verification of such a program. We identify many bugs in the implementation and write a new version that is more predictable, provably correct, and recovers more packets.
3. Along the way, we formalize in Coq several more general networking concepts: IP and UDP packets, a well-studied metric for measuring packet reordering, and sequence number arithmetic; the latter two are particularly useful for reasoning about end-to-end network functions that use timeouts.

Our proofs are available at https://github.com/verified-network-toolchain/ Verified-FEC/tree/end-to-end/proofs/FEC.

2   Background – Verification Techniques

Software verification often proceeds in layers; rather than proving desired properties directly about the source program, one writes a simpler *functional model* of the program, proves properties about this model, and separately proves that the implementation refines this model. This approach is modular: the two proofs, often requiring very different kinds of reasoning, are kept separate, and multiple low-level implementations can be proved correct against the same functional model without repetition of the high-level proofs. If the two proofs are performed in the same system, they can compose top-to-bottom to give a single theorem. This approach has been used to interactively verify distributed systems [14], an HTTP key-value server [30], a pseudorandom number generator [27], and an ODE solver [15], among others.

Alternatively, more automated verification efforts, including for networks, typically omit one of these steps: either they prove that the implementation correctly refines the model, but don't prove important properties of the model, or they prove that the model has the correct high-level properties but don't connect the abstract model to an implementation.

Most network function verification – the verification of individual network components like firewalls and load balancers – focuses on verifying that the program correctly implements a functional model and treats these models as the high-level specification [21, 28, 29]. They enable automation by heavily restricting the use of state, encapsulating specific data structures in custom libraries (see Sect. 9 for more detail). Verifying properties of entire networks [8, 13, 32] involves using simpler models tractable for fully automated verification tools like SMT solvers without verifying implementations.

Many end-to-end network functions make heavy use of state and require sophisticated higher-level reasoning, including both complex invariants describing the relationship between the state and the input/output packet streams, as well as mathematical reasoning in the domain of interest; for instance, the error-correction algorithm in the system we verify is based on linear algebra over finite fields. Proving the correctness of an implementation further involves reasoning about memory, integer overflow, and undefined behavior (we do not prove all this, but we describe how it could be done in Sect. 8.4). Therefore, we need a tool capable of reasoning at all of these levels; we use the Coq interactive theorem prover, a higher-order, dependently typed logic that is widely used in software verification, formalized mathematics, and programming language research. Coq has a large ecosystem of libraries in a variety of domains that makes proofs about functional models possible [4], as well as libraries to connect high-level proofs with low-level code, such as the Verified Software Toolchain (VST) [5] that enables sound reasoning in Coq about C programs.

```
                                              function POPPACKET
                                                 p ← s.head
      function ADDPACKET(p)                         if p.timeout ≥ currTime()  or
         if p.seqNum ≥ e then                    p.seqNum = e then
            insert(p, s);                              e ← p.seqNum + 1;
            p.timeout ← currTime() + t               forward p; popPacket
         end if                                   end if
      end function                             end function

                          global e, s
                          function MAIN
                             while true do
                                p ← receive(); addPacket(p); popPacket
                             end while
                          end function
```

Fig. 1. A simple packet reorderer with intended invariants (1) s is sorted by sequence number and (2) all sequence numbers in s are at least e, but arithmetic mod 2^{32} results in a gap between intention and reality

3   Specifying End-to-End Network Functions

To further illustrate the challenges involved when specifying end-to-end network functions, we consider a hypothetical simplified packet reorderer (Fig. 1). The reorderer keeps a list s of packets sorted by sequence number and the index e of the next expected sequence number; on arrival addPacket(p) adds the input packet p to s, and popPacket forwards in-order and timed-out packets, updating e.

Even this simple program is trickier to specify than it may appear. A natural specification is that all packets outputted by popPacket are from the sender and appear in sorted order. However, even this illustrates many of the challenges we will face in writing such a specification and proving that the program satisfies it:

1. This specification depends on the entire *stream* of sent and received packets. The output of a single call to popPacket cannot be specified except in reference to the larger stream.
2. To prove the program correct against this specification, we need to maintain invariants about the state (Fig. 1), which may themselves depend on previously sent or received packets.
3. Such a reorderer may run for a long enough time for sequence numbers to wrap around (violating the intended invariants).
4. Even with all of the above, this is a very weak spec: an implementation that dropped every packet could satisfy it. If we additionally wanted a guarantee about packets being returned, we would need to reason both about packet loss and about how many packets arrive before timing out; this depends on the amount of delay, reordering, and duplication in the network.

We will address each of these issues in the context of a packet error-correction system; many of our methods and formalizations are applicable to more general end-to-end network functions.

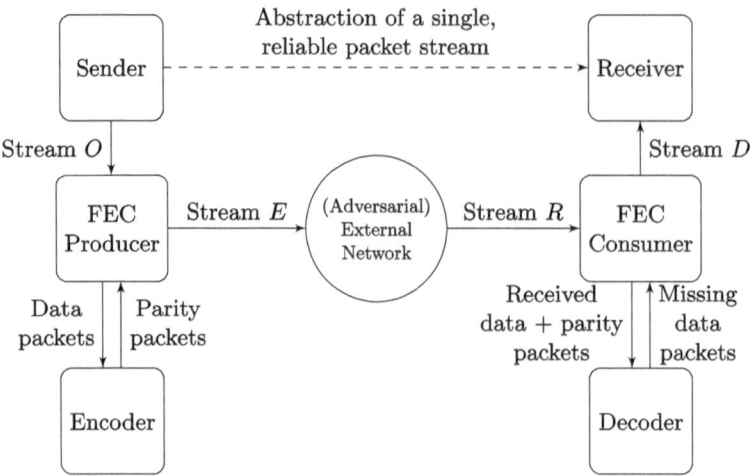

Fig. 2. FEC System Architecture

4   A Packet Error-Correction System

Often, networks deal with loss by retransmitting lost data, but in many cases, this is expensive or impossible (e.g., due to latency requirements or limited storage at the sender). Instead, one can use an *error-correcting code*, carefully encoding the data to introduce some redundancy, which allows the original data to be recovered even with some loss. In networks, this technique is known as *Forward Error Correction* (FEC).

We verify an FEC implementation developed by Bellcore (now Peraton Labs) based on Reed-Solomon coding [22]. The core encoding/decoding algorithm [17] was developed about 25 years ago;[1] the buffer- and packet-management system is about 8 years old. The program is written in C and has been used in various networking projects to support resilient communication, most recently in the DARPA EdgeCT program. We use an existing implementation rather than writing our own to show how our methods can be used to derive specifications from existing but unspecified code, to demonstrate that such analysis can find bugs in real code, and to explain how we can improve the code to create a new program that is simpler, more reliable, more efficient, and correct.

The program architecture is shown in Fig. 2. We identify four streams of packets given as inputs and outputs to different parts of the system; our specification will reference these streams. The Sender (some higher-level application) sends a stream of packets (the original stream O) to the FEC Producer, which calls the Encoder to produce parity packets. The received data packets and the generated parity packets are both sent over the network as the encoded stream E. Here, there may be some adversary or other conditions in the network causing loss, delay, reordering, and/or duplication. This results in the received stream R

---
[1] See Cohen, et al. [12] for a more detailed history of this algorithm.

(some subset of E with reordering and duplication) arriving at the FEC Consumer, which calls the Decoder to reconstruct missing packets. The resulting decoded stream D is sent to the Receiver. The Sender and Receiver (and any other higher-level applications) believe that they are communicating with each other over a mostly reliable connection.

The FEC system can be broken into two pieces: the Encoder/Decoder, which implements the Reed-Solomon erasure code to determine the parities and reconstruct missing packets, and the Producer/Consumer, which sends and receives packets and decides which packets to send to the Encoder/Decoder to recover missing data. The Reed-Solomon code is a *block code* – it encodes a batch of k packets, producing h parity packets such that if at least k of these $k + h$ total packets are received, the Decoder can recover all packets in the batch. Accordingly, the Producer receives packets and forwards them along, marking each with some metadata to identify their batch and their data/parity status and storing copies of these packets until k have been received, at which point it calls the Encoder to produce parities, outputting the result. The Consumer groups incoming packets into their batches and calls the Decoder when k packets in a batch have been received. It also periodically times out stored batches to prevent long search times and limit memory usage.

5   Developing a High-Level Specification

Any attempt to develop a specification for this system immediately encounters all of the challenges described in Sect. 3, though the stored state is much more complicated and the timeout mechanism much less predictable than for the simple reorderer (Sect. 5.1). Comments in the existing C code indicate that the program was supposed to handle loss, reordering, duplication, and delay; our spec must account for these as well.

5.1   Implementation-Specific Behavior

Beyond the considerations in Sect. 3, efforts to formulate a spec for this FEC implementation encounter two additional challenges. First, there is no "natural" specification; it is entirely unclear what such a system should guarantee. FEC cannot guarantee packet recovery if too many packets are dropped, so the program might be expected to provide some guarantees on recovery in a well-behaved network environment or it may operate in a best-effort fashion to attempt to recover as much data as possible.

Second, the program as written does not satisfy any reasonable spec. Formally, we cannot yet call this a bug, as the program makes no guarantees about its behavior; indeed, part of our motivation in giving a formal spec is to be able to concretely identify bugs. Yet in the course of attempting to derive a specification from the code, we discovered (and fixed, see Sect. 7) many problems, which we grouped into 3 categories: The first consists of issues that should be considered bugs under any reasonable specification.

1. The code leaks memory. Some of the memory leaks are acknowledged by the code's comments; others are not. Due to the unpredictable timeout mechanism (see below), the data structure to store the batches in the Consumer can grow arbitrarily large even in "nice" cases (e.g. all the packet arrive in order).
2. The code implicitly (and seemingly unintentionally) casts between signed and unsigned ints.

The second category consists of behaviors that could cause a serious problem: hallucinatory "reconstruction" of packets that were never sent.

3. The program does not handle sequence number (and integer) wraparound correctly; it uses ordinary integer comparison rather than serial number arithmetic [10]. If enough packets arrive, it can group packets into batches incorrectly, producing garbage packets that are "recovered" and sent to the Receiver. This is a problem if program handles packet streams with more than $2^{31} - 1$ packets,[2] which is a fairly small number of packets at current network speeds.

The third category consists of behaviors that cause the program to fail to recover all packets it could plausibly recover.

4. The implementation does not call the Decoder unless the kth packet received in a batch is a parity packet; thus, with even a small amount of reordering, a recoverable batch can be ignored.
5. With only small amounts of reordering, the Consumer ignores the received packet, forwarding it to the Receiver without storing it.
6. Timeouts are handled inconsistently and unpredictably.

They not only prevent us from giving guarantees about the recovered packets, but violate any notion of *locality* about packet-batches – that is, whether a batch is recovered does not only depend on the packets in that batch. In particular, both of the following can occur:

7. An input packet can be forwarded without being stored if some *other* batch has timed out.
8. In other cases, batches that should time out do not, as long as no packet from a later batch arrives. This, tiny changes in reordering and/or delay can change whether a batch is recovered.

5.2 Layers of Specification

How then, should we formulate a specification so as to capture which of these behaviors should be regarded as bugs? We are interested in knowing both *what guarantees the program gives in good scenarios* (defining these appropriately) as well as *how bad things can be in bad/adversarial ones*. Our approach is to

---

[2] This implementation uses a custom sequence number that counts packets, not bytes.

design different layers of specification based on various assumptions about the external environment. For the FEC system, we first want the following under all circumstances:

Property 1. The program does not crash, leak memory, access invalid memory, have signed integer overflow, or use undefined behavior.

Under this spec, items 1 and 2 in the above list are definitely bugs. We note that unsigned integer overflow (carry) is expected due to sequence numbers; we explicitly account for this below.

Next, we identify two properties which must hold to give the following principle: the higher-level Sender/Receiver should never be worse off for having used FEC (as opposed to just sending packets and accepting loss). The FEC system should not drop any packets that are correctly sent and received, and it should not create any invalid packets that were not originally sent:

Property 2. Suppose a data packet (i.e., a packet from stream O) is in the received stream R. Then it is in the decoded stream D.

Property 3. Every packet in the decoded stream D is in the original stream O.

Property 3 does *not* hold of the current implementation due to bug 3 above. To rule out sequence number wraparound, we need some assumption about the environment. To fix this, we change the program to use 64-bit sequence numbers and assume that no more than $2^{63} - 1$ packets are sent.[3] Additionally, we need serial number arithmetic for other comparisons that could be affected by wraparound.

Thus, we have two levels of specification: the FEC system should *always* satisfy Properties 1 and 2, and if at most $2^{63} - 1$ packets are sent, it satisfies Property 3 (of course, it will satisfy Property 3 in other settings as well, but we do not prove this). These properties claim that even in adversarial network conditions, the FEC system will not do anything too bad. But this spec is still quite weak; even a system that did nothing but forward data packets and ignore parities could satisfy it. We want to give a stronger spec – one that guarantees, under "normal" network conditions, that the FEC system actually ensures reliable delivery by recovering lost packets.

We expect the ith batch to be recovered under the following condition:

Condition 1. k and h are fixed for all packets. $0 \leq i \leq \frac{|O|}{k}$, and at least k packets of the $k + h$ packets between position $i(k + h)$ and $(i + 1)(k + h)$ in stream E appear in stream R.[4]

---

[3] This is a safe assumption. At gigabit speeds, even if each packet were only 1 bit, wraparound would only occur after 250 years. Alternatively, we could assume weak bounds on reordering, duplication, etc. to ensure that sequence numbers are never ambiguous. But we would like Property 3 to hold under *any* network behavior.

[4] This loss condition is not ideal: it reveals the batch structure of the FEC algorithm. However, other formulations (for example, that k out of every $k + h$ consecutive packets are received) are overly restrictive or do not correctly capture the condition.

We would like to say something like the following:

Property 4. Suppose that Condition 1 holds for i. Then packets ik to $(i + 1)k$ from stream O appear in D.

In other words, if the FEC parameters are fixed and no more than k packets in the batch are lost, then all packets in this batch are received by the Receiver. It immediately follows from this property that if *all* batches are recoverable (no more than k packets in each batch are lost), then all packets are received. Combined with Property 3, this implies that streams O and D have exactly the same packets. But Property 4 does not hold unconditionally: a batch can timeout before it is recovered; furthermore, bugs 3–6 cause violations of this property even if a particular batch did not timeout. Our next step is therefore to determine assumptions under which Property 4 holds, which involves detailed reasoning about the external network environment.

6   Formalizing Properties of Packet Streams

To prove that the FEC program actually recovers certain batches, we need a way to state that all packets in a batch arrive before timing out. In other words, we need the notion that packets sent at similar times from the Producer (close together in E) should arrive within some specified time interval at the Consumer (reasonably close together in R). This is not unique to FEC; any end-to-end program with timeouts and operating on groups of elements will need similar reasoning.

But reasoning about this is difficult: packets can be delayed, dropped, reordered, and duplicated, so we cannot assume direct relationships between a packet's position in E and its position in R. Instead, we will quantify and formalize well-studied, empirical metrics for each of these features and prove that under reasonable bounds on these metrics, batches will not be timed out before they are completed. Since timeouts serve the purpose of identifying exceptional circumstances under which we should *not* expect some packets to be received, this approach makes sense; if the external network behaves reasonably, timeouts should not prevent otherwise recoverable batches from being recovered. To ensure this, we will modify the program's timeout mechanism along the way to simplify it and ensure locality.

6.1   Reordering

Measuring packet reordering is a well-studied problem; metrics for doing so are summarized in RFCs 4737 [18] and 5236 [24]. Some metrics count the number of reordered packets; other quantify the extent of the reordering, which is more useful to us. One such metric is Reorder Density (RD) [7,20], which measures the *displacement* of each packet, or the difference between the packet's arrival position and its position in the correctly ordered stream, ignoring duplicates.

In a comparative study, RD compared favorably to a variety of other reordering metrics on its robustness to packet loss and duplication, ability to capture reordering, usefulness in evaluating network behavior, time and space complexity, and more [19]; the same study found that reordering events are frequent but small. This validates our approach; most reordering is quite small, so we can safely assume a bound on the maximum displacement that the vast majority of packet streams will satisfy.

$seq[i]$	1	2	3	6	4	5	7
$RI[i]$	1	2	3	4	5	6	7
$d[i]$	0	0	0	−2	1	1	0

$seq[i]$	1	4	3	5	3	8	7	6
$RI[i]$	1	3	4	5	x	6	7	8
$d[i]$	0	−1	1	0	x	−2	0	2

Fig. 3. Reorder Density (RD) (a) without and (b) with duplicates and drops

Figure 3 shows how RD is computed: the input sequence is compared with the Receive Index (RI) sequence, indicating the in-order arrivals; these values are subtracted to get the displacement (d) of each packet. Duplicate packets are ignored; they have no d or RI value, and dropped packets are skipped in the RI sequence. We choose RD as our reordering metric and we will assume a bound d on the displacement of each packet between the sent stream E and the received stream R. Section 8.3 discusses our formalization of RD in Coq.

6.2   Duplication and Timeouts

Bounds on reordering help us prove that packets in the same batch are received before the batch times out by quantifying how many packets can arrive in between packets in the same batch. However, duplicate packets cause problems: not only could arbitrarily many packets arrive in the middle of a batch (without a further bound), but reordering metrics like RD intentionally ignore duplication.

Metrics for duplication are sparse; RFC 5560 [23] defines a metric that simply counts the number of occurrences of each packet, but it is unclear if this metric has ever been empirically studied. We instead care about how spread out packets can be, so we use the following condition: there is a bound m such that any two duplicate packets in R have at most m packets between them. This is inspired by RD: if we imagine duplicate packets as two different packets sent from the sender in sequence, then this metric is very close to difference between their displacements.

To reason about timeouts, we must combine the assumed bounds on reordering and duplicates with an assumption about the arrival times of packets close together in R. But this is indirect and unsatisfactory: it depends on network speeds and congestion, and does not allow the Producer to pause between batches. Moreover, reasoning about duplication and reordering together is difficult; this approach results in only weak, multiplicative bounds. Instead, we argue that the timeout mechanism should be changed: instead of measuring in seconds, we should count *the number of unique packets received.* This choice improves the program, the spec, and the proofs in several ways. The sender is allowed to wait between packet arrivals or batches; the condition does not depend on network speeds or system time (making the Consumer a pure function of the packet inputs). Moreover, this improves efficiency: the program already checks for duplicate packets, but now the size of the data structures can be bounded exactly; they also do not depend on network speeds. Finally, reasoning is much simpler: RD is naturally expressed in terms of unique packets; aligning our timeout mechanism with this allows us to reason about reordering and duplication separately and give stronger, additive bounds (Sect. 8.3).

With all of these features in mind, we can write our final strong spec, first specifying the bounds on the external conditions and some parameters to prevent overflow.

Condition 2. The following bounds hold:

1. For all packets, the displacement between E and R is bounded by d.
2. Any two identical packets in R have at most m packets between them.
3. The timeout threshold is at least $k + h + 2d + m$.

Condition 3. The timeout threshold is smaller than 2^{31}, all sequence numbers are unique and less than 2^{63}, $0 < k \leq 127$, and $0 < h \leq 128$.[5]

Property 5. Suppose Conditions 2 and 3 hold and Condition 1 holds for i. Then all packets in batch i (packets ik to $(i + 1)k$ in O) appear in D.

This specification tells us that the program guarantees recovery of certain packets under reasonable network conditions. Now, we have two tasks: correct the program's bugs so that it satisfies Properties 1, 2, 3, and 5 and then prove that this is the case.

7   A New Program

To fix the problems described in Sect. 5.1, we make some modifications to the source program:

- We fix the memory leaks resulting from the lack of free after malloc.
- We use 64-bit sequence numbers instead of 32-bit ones (Sect. 5.1).
- For all sequence number comparisons (including the batch ID numbers, which are based on the first packet's sequence number), we use serial number arithmetic (Sect. 8.3), which handles wraparound correctly.
- In the Consumer, we change the timeout mechanism to count unique packet arrivals rather than seconds (Sect. 6.2). In reality, this is an estimate (packets may have timed out, causing duplicates to be identified as unique); we account for this in our correctness proofs (Sect. 8).

---

[5] The k and h bounds arise from the FEC algorithm.

– Finally, we completely change the timeout mechanism. Before, the Consumer only timed out batches if a packet from a previous batch (before the latest) arrived, it only ever timed out a single batch, and it violated locality as described in Sect. 5.1. The new implementation iterates through the entire list after each arrival, deleting all timed-out batches.

With these changes, the system is more reliable, more predictable, and recovers more packets. However, the new timeout mechanism seemingly reduces the performance, adding iteration through the batch list each time. But this is not necessarily the case. Before, the batch list could be arbitrarily long, and thus a single iteration could take much longer (even in typical cases, such as a packet arriving in the batch immediately preceding the latest). More importantly, the lack of iteration in the previous implementation was really a bug, both because it led to space leaks and because the unpredictable timeout mechanism made the system recover fewer packets than it otherwise could have. This would degrade the performance further if retransmissions were required to recover these missing packets. Finally, we note that our new approach could be implemented efficiently with the right data structures: a hash table to identify the batch and a priority queue to remove old batches would reduce the time per arrival to logarithmic in the number of batches, which itself is kept quite small with the new timeout mechanism.

8 Proving the Program Correct

8.1 Functional Models and Data Structures

As Sect. 2 describes, we create a functional model of the program, which we prove correct according to the various high-level specs (Properties 1, 2, 3, and 5; we mainly focus here on Property 5). Our models are functional programs in Coq, one Coq function closely matching each C function. We use machine-length integers and data structures closely mirroring those in the C program. The models of the Producer and Consumer take as input some internal state, the current packet, and some external state, returning the updated internal state and a list of output packets; from this, we define iterated versions that input and output packet streams, updating the internal state with each arrival.

Representing the state of each function is a crucial ingredient in our proofs. The Producer and Consumer operate over streams of packets, passing appropriate batches to the core Encoder/Decoder; to link these streams together, we introduce a Block data type, which bundles together the data and parity packets in a batch (using our separate formalization of IP and UDP packets) along with additional metadata (batch ID, FEC k and h values, etc.). This abstraction serves two purposes: we can reason about the state of each function in a similar way (the Producer stores an option Block, and the Consumer stores a list Block, each representing the batch(es) in progress) and we can view the E and R packet streams alternatively as a stream of Blocks satisfying particular invariants. This allows us to reason about the Producer and Consumer separately and provides a common view of the inputs, outputs, and internal state.

8.2   Linking the Producer and Consumer

The Block abstraction helps us in the following way: the Producer maintains a currently-in-progress Block; when a batch is complete, it clears its internal state and begins the next batch. Thus, the Blocks comprising the stream E consist of those formed by the Producer. Meanwhile, the Blocks in stream R are *subblocks* of those from E – since packets may be dropped but no new packets can be created. The internal state of the Consumer stores the currently-in-progress batches as Blocks, each of which is a subblock of a Block from R (some packets may be dropped due to timeouts). Therefore, our basic proof strategy is to prove properties of the Blocks in E by proving invariants about the internal state of the Producer, then proving that these properties hold of subblocks and therefore hold of the Consumer's state as well.

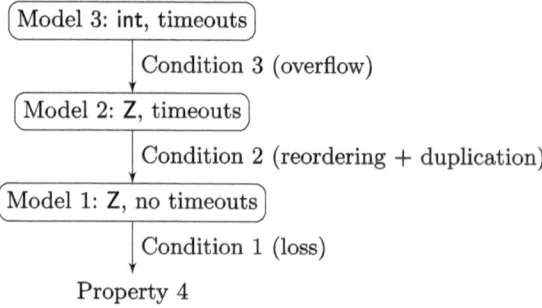

Fig. 4. Consumer Refinement Proofs

For example, the Consumer calls the Reed-Solomon Decoder on a batch when it receives k packets. For the operation to be valid, all packets from k to $k + h$ in the batch must be parity packets produced by the Reed-Solomon Encoder from some input data consistent with the received data packets (packets 0 to $k - 1$ in the batch). Then, the Decoder will recover the original input (proved in Coq in [12]). We prove that the Blocks stored in the Consumer have this structure (which we call *well-formed*) by showing that the Producer creates a batch by appropriately calling the Reed-Solomon Encoder and that subblocks remain well-formed.

8.3   The Consumer

The Consumer is complicated, and its proofs must reason about the Decoder correctness, sequence number wraparound, and timeouts. To handle this cleanly, we use a refinement-based approach, writing 3 layers of functional models (Fig. 4). Model 1 uses mathematical (unbounded) integers and has no timeouts; under the loss assumptions, we prove that it satisfies Property 4. Model 2 adds timeouts; we prove that under the reordering and duplication bounds, it is equivalent to

Model 1. Model 3 uses machine-length integers and serial number arithmetic; we prove that under the bounds assumptions for sequence numbers and the timeout threshold, it is equivalent to Model 2. We compose all of these proofs to show that Property 5 holds of Model 3.

The Consumer with No Timeouts. Proving Model 1 correct follows from the observation that, with no timeouts, the Blocks stored in the Consumer's state are *exactly* the blocks of the received stream R. By the loss assumption, the ith batch has at least k packets in the stream, so when the kth packet arrives, the Consumer will call the Reed-Solomon Decoder and (by the well-formedness result above and [12]), output the missing data packets. There is some subtlety; the Block abstraction is useful for avoiding reasoning about reordering and duplication when not needed, as it only notes the presence of a packet, not its location in the stream. Thus, to lift our location-based loss condition (Condition 1) to the Block level, we show that packets $i(k+h)$ to $(i+1)(k+h)$ in E comprise exactly the packets of some block in E.

The Consumer with Timeouts. With timeouts, it is no longer the case that the Consumer's blocks are those of R; instead, each is a subblock of a block from R (and thus of a block from E). To prove Models 1 and 2 equivalent, we show that the bounds on reordering and duplication imply that all packets in a batch arrive before the batch times out. We first formalize the Reorder Density metric (Sect. 6.1) in Coq. Since this metric ignores duplicates, we can express it naturally via the sent and received packet streams with duplicates removed. This fits very nicely with our packet-based timeout mechanism; a packet's arrival time is its index in deduplicated received packet stream. Thus, we can relate the RI and diplacement values directly with the timing mechanism and show the following:

Theorem 1. *Consider sent and received packet lists E and R, with no duplicates in E, and suppose that the displacements of all arriving packets are bounded by d. Then if packets p_1 and p_2 are separated by at most n packets in E, they are separated by at most $n + 2d$ unique packets in R.*

This theorem is intuitive – the worst case is that each packet moves d spaces in the "opposite" direction – but is nontrivial to show; it requires reasoning about the precise relationship between RI, displacement, and sequence numbers. However, the duplication case is independent and much simpler:

Theorem 2. *Suppose that at most m packets appear between any pair of duplicates in R. Suppose that p_1 and p_2 are separated by at most n packets in E and that p_1 arrives before p_2 in R. Then, p_2 arrives at most $n + m$ timesteps after p_1.*

These theorems imply a bound on our timeout threshold: any value at least $k + h + 2d + m$ suffices, where k and h are the FEC parameters, d is the displacement bound, and m is the duplication bound. This bound is additive rather than multiplicative and thus much tighter than those achievable with the time-based timeout mechanism. In practice, k and h are often smaller than 10, d has rarely exceeded 50 in real-world tests [7,19] (though these studies are 15–20 years old – higher network speeds may result in higher displacements), and m is not measured but seems likely to be no larger than d (we would expect more reordering than duplication in practice). Thus, a threshold of a few hundred packets is likely sufficient to handle normal network conditions; our proofs are all parametric in the choice of threshold.

With these results, we prove by a series of invariants that Model 2 never times out blocks that have packets yet to arrive; this implies that its output is the same as Model 1.

Machine and Sequence Number Arithmetic. Finally, for our machine-length-integer version, we formalize Serial Number Arithmetic from RFC 1982 [10] and prove it correct. We can define serial number comparison efficiently with the following C function:[6]

```
int seq_cmp(unsigned int i1, unsigned int i2) { return ((int)(i1−i2)); }
```

a is considered smaller than b if seq_cmp(a, b) is negative, equal if zero, and larger otherwise. In this definition, integers close to each other (within 2^{31}) are comparable, with the expected behavior (e.g., $2^{32} - 1 < 0$). To formalize this in Coq, we define functions seq_lt, seq_eq, seq_gt that compute the appropriate comparisons, and we prove the theorem:

Theorem 3. *Let* repr *be the function that gives the 32-bit representation of an integer (i.e., z mod 2^{32}). Let z_1 and z_2 be unbounded integers such that $|z_1 - z_2| < 2^{31}$. Then,* seq_lt(repr($z1$),repr($z2$)) $= true \iff z1 < z2$.

In other words, given two integers close to each other, sequence number comparison correctly decides which is smaller, even with wraparound (and likewise for the other two functions). With these results, formalized using CompCert's [16] machine-length integer Coq library, we show that all sequence number comparisons are performed between unsigned integers whose values are within 2^{31} (this results in the 2^{30} upper bound on the timeout threshold); hence, by Theorem 3, all uses of serial number arithmetic exactly correspond to unbounded integer comparison and therefore Models 2 and 3 are equivalent.

Finally, we compose all 3 layers and the Producer proofs to prove a single theorem about the machine-length functional model;[7] this model should exactly correspond to the C program's behavior:

---

[6] We use 32-bit as an example; our proofs are generic and we also need the 64-bit case.
[7] The Producer only compares integers between 0 and 256; wraparound is impossible.

Theorem 4. *Suppose Conditions 2 and 3 hold and Condition 1 holds for i. Then, packets ik to $(i+1)k$ in O appear in D, the decoded stream formed by the Producer and Model 3 of the Consumer.*

This theorem provides guarantees even if particular batches are unrecoverable. If all batches are recoverable, we have the following:

Corollary 1. *Suppose Conditions 2 and 3 hold, Condition 1 holds for all $0 \leq i \leq \frac{|O|}{k}$, and k divides $|O|$. Then all packets in O appear in D.*

8.4 From Coq to C Code

From here, we could use the Verified Software Toolchain (VST) [5] to prove that the C code refines our machine-length functional model, composing the proofs with our functional-model proofs above. VST is proved sound with respect to the CompCert verified C compiler [16], so our proofs would hold down to the assembly-language level. Additionally, this would also show that the program is free of memory leaks, undefined behavior, or I/O beyond what is written in the specification. This approach is feasible for verifying real C code [3,12,27], and we designed our functional model to adhere closely to the C code and be verifiable with VST, for instance using CompCert's machine-length integers.

We did not carry on our verification down to the C code, as our primary focus was in developing tools for specifying and reasoning about end-to-end network functions at a higher level. We note that even without a VST proof, we identified and fixed many bugs in our target program, leading to simpler, more predictable, and correct code, demonstrating that formal specification and verification techniques are useful even partially applied.

9   Related Work

As discussed in Sect. 2, most previous network verification efforts take one of two approaches, both of which are orthogonal to our work. *Network verification* models a network as a simpler abstraction, proving properties with SMT solvers and other automated methods. Some recent work on control plane verification includes Minesweeper [9], Tiramisu [1], Hoyan [26], SRE [32] and Timepiece [2]. In the data plane, verification tools include Katra [8] and Flash [13]. *Network function verification* develops verified per-packet network function implementations (NAT, firewall, load balancer, etc.); examples include VigNAT [29], Vigor [28], Klint [21], and Gravel [31]. While these network functions can maintain state updated on packet arrival, this use is restricted to particular data structures separately (interactively) verified against a functional specification or axiomatized using SMT formulas. These restrictions, and others on the presensece of loops, pointers, and the overall program structure, enable automation. Crucially, the specifications treat these data structures as abstract, enabling reasoning about how an individual packet interacts with them but not about how this state relates to previous packets.

Other work has focused on verifying transport-layer components. Cluzel, et al. [11] verify a TCP implementation by translating to SPARK., verifying against the protocol expressed as a state machine – the reasoning is still per-packet, since they do not prove higher-level reliability guarantees. Arun, et al. [6] verify congestion control algorithms against first-order logic specifications using SMT solvers; they prove higher-level properties, and the SMT-outputted packet traces may include duplicates and timeouts. Beyond network components, Verdi [25] is a Coq library to verify distributed systems; it allows the user to define the assumed network environment, including reordering, duplication, loss, and time-outs; however, this controls the presence, not the extent, of these effects.

10 Conclusion and Future Work

Formally specifying and verifying end-to-end network functions involves numerous challenges, many of which are widely applicable to other real-world programs. Specifications may be unclear, dependent on external conditions, and more complicated to express than via simple inputs and outputs (as the behavior may depend on previously processed packets). We show that a layered, interactive approach can clarify assumptions, identify intended guarantees, and lead to cleaner, more predictable, provably correct code. We would like to demonstrate our methods on other end-to-end transport-layer network functions and even more general "dusty deck" programs that are underspecified and encounter similar issues. We would also like to automate some of our verification and to develop more general libraries for reasoning about external conditions like timeouts and packet reordering. We believe that our techniques are applicable to a wide variety of complex software, and we hope that formal specification and verification can become standard ways to analyze and improve real-world systems.

Acknowledgment. This material is based upon work supported by the Defense Advanced Research Projects Agency (DARPA) under Contract No. HR001120C0160.

References

1. Abhashkumar, A., Gember-Jacobson, A., Akella, A.: Tiramisu: fast multilayer network verification. In: 17th USENIX Symposium on Networked Systems Design and Implementation (NSDI 20), Santa Clara, CA, pp. 201–219. USENIX Association (2020)
2. Alberdingk Thijm, T., Beckett, R., Gupta, A., Walker, D.: Modular control plane verification via temporal invariants. Proc. ACM Program. Lang. **7**(PLDI) (2023). https://doi.org/10.1145/3591222

3. Appel, A.W.: Verification of a cryptographic primitive: SHA-256. ACM Trans. Program. Lang. Syst. **37**(2) (2015). https://doi.org/10.1145/2701415
4. Appel, A.W.: Coq's vibrant ecosystem for verification engineering (invited talk). In: Proceedings of the 11th ACM SIGPLAN International Conference on Certified Programs and Proofs. CPP 2022, New York, NY, USA, pp. 2–11. Association for Computing Machinery (2022). https://doi.org/10.1145/3497775.3503951
5. Appel, A.W., et al.: Program Logics for Certified Compilers. Cambridge University Press, Cambridge (2014)
6. Arun, V., Arashloo, M.T., Saeed, A., Alizadeh, M., Balakrishnan, H.: Toward formally verifying congestion control behavior. In: Proceedings of the 2021 ACM SIGCOMM 2021 Conference. SIGCOMM '21, New York, NY, USA, pp. 1–16. Association for Computing Machinery (2021). https://doi.org/10.1145/3452296.3472912
7. Bare, A.A., Jayasumana, A.P., Banka, T.: Metrics for degree of reordering in packet sequences. In: Proceedings LCN 2002. 27th Annual IEEE Conference on Local Computer Networks, Los Alamitos, CA, USA, p. 0333. IEEE Computer Society (2002). https://doi.org/10.1109/LCN.2002.1181802
8. Beckett, R., Gupta, A.: Katra: Realtime verification for multilayer networks. In: 19th USENIX Symposium on Networked Systems Design and Implementation (NSDI 22), pp. 617–634, Renton, WA. USENIX Association (2022)
9. Beckett, R., Gupta, A., Mahajan, R., Walker, D.: A general approach to network configuration verification. In: Proceedings of the Conference of the ACM Special Interest Group on Data Communication. SIGCOMM '17, New York, NY, USA, pp. 155–168.. Association for Computing Machinery (2017). https://doi.org/10.1145/3098822.3098834
10. Bush, R., Elz, R.: Serial Number Arithmetic. RFC 1982 (1996). https://doi.org/10.17487/RFC1982
11. Cluzel, G., Georgiou, K., Moy, Y., Zeller, C.: Layered formal verification of a TCP stack. In: 2021 IEEE Secure Development Conference (SecDev), pp. 86–93 (2021). https://doi.org/10.1109/SecDev51306.2021.00028
12. Cohen, J.M., Wang, Q., Appel, A.W.: Verified erasure correction in Coq with MathComp and VST. In: Shoham, S., Vizel, Y. (eds.) Computer Aided Verification, pp. 272–292. Springer, Cham (2022). https://doi.org/10.1007/978-3-031-13188-2_14
13. Guo, D., Chen, S., Gao, K., Xiang, Q., Zhang, Y., Yang, Y.R.: Flash: fast, consistent data plane verification for large-scale network settings. In: Proceedings of the ACM SIGCOMM 2022 Conference, pp. 314–335 (2022). https://doi.org/10.1145/3544216.3544246
14. Hawblitzel, C., et al.: Ironfleet: proving practical distributed systems correct. In: Proceedings of the 25th Symposium on Operating Systems Principles. SOSP '15, New York, NY, USA, pp. 1–17. Association for Computing Machinery (2015). https://doi.org/10.1145/2815400.2815428
15. Kellison, A.E., Appel, A.W.: Verified numerical methods for ordinary differential equations. In: Isac, O., Ivanov, R., Katz, G., Narodytska, N., Nenzi, L. (eds.) Software Verification and Formal Methods for ML-Enabled Autonomous Systems, pp. 147–163. Springer, Cham (2022). https://doi.org/10.1007/978-3-031-21222-2_9
16. Leroy, X.: Formal verification of a realistic compiler. Commun. ACM **52**(7), 107–115 (2009). https://doi.org/10.1145/1538788.1538814
17. McAuley, A.J.: Reliable broadband communication using a burst erasure correcting code. In: Proceedings of the ACM Symposium on Communications Architectures & Protocols. SIGCOMM '90, New York, NY, USA, pp. 297–306 (1990). https://doi.org/10.1145/99508.99566

18. Morton, A., Ramachandran, G., Shalunov, S., Ciavattone, L., Perser, J.: Packet Reordering Metrics. RFC 4737 (2006). https://doi.org/10.17487/RFC4737
19. Piratla, N.M., Jayasumana, A.P.: Metrics for packet reordering-a comparative analysis. Int. J. Commun. Syst. **21**(1), 99–113 (2008). https://doi.org/10.1002/dac.884
20. Piratla, N.M., Jayasumana, A.P., Bare, A.A.: Reorder density (RD): a formal, comprehensive metric for packet reordering. In: Boutaba, R., Almeroth, K., Puigjaner, R., Shen, S., Black, J.P. (eds.) NETWORKING 2005. Networking Technologies, Services, and Protocols; Performance of Computer and Communication Networks; Mobile and Wireless Communications Systems. pp. 78–89. Springer, Cham (2005). https://doi.org/10.1007/11422778_7
21. Pirelli, S., Valentukonytė, A., Argyraki, K., Candea, G.: Automated verification of network function binaries. In: 19th USENIX Symposium on Networked Systems Design and Implementation (NSDI 22), Renton, WA, pp. 585–600. USENIX Association (2022)
22. Reed, I.S., Solomon, G.: Polynomial codes over certain finite fields. J. Soc. Ind. Appl. Math. **8**(2), 300–304 (1960). https://doi.org/10.1137/0108018
23. Uijterwaal, D.H.A.: A One-Way Packet Duplication Metric. RFC 5560 (2009). https://doi.org/10.17487/RFC5560
24. Whitner, R., Banka, T., Piratla, N.M., Bare, A.A., Jayasumana, P.A.P.: Improved Packet Reordering Metrics. RFC 5236 (2008). https://doi.org/10.17487/RFC5236
25. Wilcox, J.R., et al.: Verdi: a framework for implementing and formally verifying distributed systems. In: Proceedings of the 36th ACM SIGPLAN Conference on Programming Language Design and Implementation. PLDI '15, New York, NY, USA, pp. 357–368. Association for Computing Machinery (2015). https://doi.org/10.1145/2737924.2737958
26. Ye, F., et al.: Accuracy, scalability, coverage: a practical configuration verifier on a global wan. In: Proceedings of the Annual Conference of the ACM Special Interest Group on Data Communication on the Applications, Technologies, Architectures, and Protocols for Computer Communication. SIGCOMM '20, New York, NY, USA, pp. 599–614. Association for Computing Machinery (2020). https://doi.org/10.1145/3387514.3406217
27. Ye, K.Q., Green, M., Sanguansin, N., Beringer, L., Petcher, A., Appel, A.W.: Verified correctness and security of MbedTLS HMAC-DRBG. In: Proceedings of the 2017 ACM SIGSAC Conference on Computer and Communications Security. CCS '17, New York, NY, USA, pp. 2007–2020 (2017). https://doi.org/10.1145/3133956.3133974
28. Zaostrovnykh, A., et al.: Verifying software network functions with no verification expertise. In: Proceedings of the 27th ACM Symposium on Operating Systems Principles. SOSP '19, New York, NY, USA, pp. 275–290 (2019). https://doi.org/10.1145/3341301.3359647
29. Zaostrovnykh, A., Pirelli, S., Pedrosa, L., Argyraki, K., Candea, G.: A formally verified NAT. In: Proceedings of the Conference of the ACM Special Interest Group on Data Communication. SIGCOMM '17, New York, NY, USA, pp. 141–154 (2017). doi: https://doi.org/10.1145/3098822.3098833
30. Zhang, H., et al.: Verifying an HTTP key-value server with interaction trees and VST. In: Cohen, L., Kaliszyk, C. (eds.) 12th International Conference on Interactive Theorem Proving (ITP 2021). Leibniz International Proceedings in Informatics (LIPIcs), vol. 193, pp. 32:1–32:19. Schloss Dagstuhl – Leibniz-Zentrum für Informatik, Dagstuhl, Germany (2021). https://doi.org/10.4230/LIPIcs.ITP.2021.32

31. Zhang, K., Zhuo, D., Akella, A., Krishnamurthy, A., Wang, X.: Automated verification of customizable middlebox properties with Gravel. In: 17th USENIX Symposium on Networked Systems Design and Implementation (NSDI 20), Santa Clara, CA, pp. 221–239. USENIX Association (2020)
32. Zhang, P., Wang, D., Gember-Jacobson, A.: Symbolic router execution. In: Proceedings of the ACM SIGCOMM 2022 Conference. SIGCOMM '22, New York, NY, USA, pp. 336–349. Association for Computing Machinery (2022). https://doi.org/10.1145/3544216.3544264

Formally Verified ZTA Requirements for OT/ICS Environments with Isabelle/HOL

Yakoub Nemouchi[✉][iD], Sriharsha Etigowni, Alexander Zolan[iD], and Richard Macwan

National Renewable Energy Laboratory, Golden, CO, USA
{yakoub.nemouchi,sriharsha.etigowni,alexander.zolan}@nrel.gov

Abstract. The clean energy transformation includes the integration of distributed energy resources with the power grid, which has led to a substantial increase in the complexity of power grids infrastructure and the underlying operational technology environment. Power grids infrastructure represents an operational technology environment that has become a system of systems, integrating heterogeneous devices which are both software-and hardware-intensive; as a result, there are increasing demands to exploit advances in the commodity of software-hardware infrastructures to improve energy systems requirements such as cybersecurity and resilience. In such a setting, system requirements at different levels mix, which leads to vulnerabilities and undesirable outcomes. The use of formal methods to characterize and prove system requirements removes ambiguity, increases automation, and provides high levels of assurance and reliability. In this paper, we contribute a methodology and a framework for the system-level verification of zero trust architecture requirements in operational technology environments. We define a formal specification for the core functionalities of operational technology environments, the corresponding invariants, and security proofs. Of particular note is our modular approach for the formal verification of asynchronous interactions in operational technology environments. The formal specification and the proofs have been mechanized using the interactive theorem proving environment Isabelle/HOL.

Keywords: formal methods · Isabelle/HOL · OT security · microgrids

1 Introduction

Operational technology (OT) environments are used to integrate, monitor, and enforce control actions in industrial control systems (ICSs) [43]. OT environments include devices such as supervisory control and data acquisition (SCADA) systems, programmable logic controllers (PLCs), intelligent electronic devices (IEDs), and remote terminal units (RTUs) [56], each of which can be connected to a distributed control network infrastructure featuring Lightweight Directory Access Protocol (LDAP) servers, routers, and firewalls [20]. The ongoing transition to renewable energy systems provides a new dimension of security risks to the OT landscape [48]. The next generation of OT environments will integrate distributed energy resources (DERs), which are broadly defined to include (i) microturbines and other combustion technologies [45],

© The Author(s), under exclusive license to Springer Nature Switzerland AG 2024
A. Reynolds and S. Tasiran (Eds.): VSTTE 2023, LNCS 14095, pp. 64–84, 2024.
https://doi.org/10.1007/978-3-031-66064-1_5

(ii) wind plants [35], (iii) solar energy plants [57], (iv) smart buildings [49], (v) electrical vehicles (EVs) [23], (vi) fuel cells [46], and (vii) other kinds of hybrid systems [41]. A microgrid configuration can comprise one or more of items (i)–(vi) [28]. These critical and software-intensive cyber-physical systems (CPSs) [42,55] contain OT/ICS devices that are interconnected with each other, with the internet, with the environment, with the energy infrastructure, and with other critical infrastructure and key resources [31], which can lead to a large collection of entry points for cyberattacks [22]. CPSs can create domains of *mixed criticalities* [5], wherein system requirements of different levels mix. In such a setting, undesirable outcomes are more likely to occur, highlighting a need to increase the level of assurance and reliability for OT environments. Our proposed solution combines the use of known security architectures, such as the zero trust architecture (ZTA) [27], with the use of formal methods (FMs) [29], the latter of which provides assurance evidence with an absolute guarantee that an OT environment meets ZTA requirements.

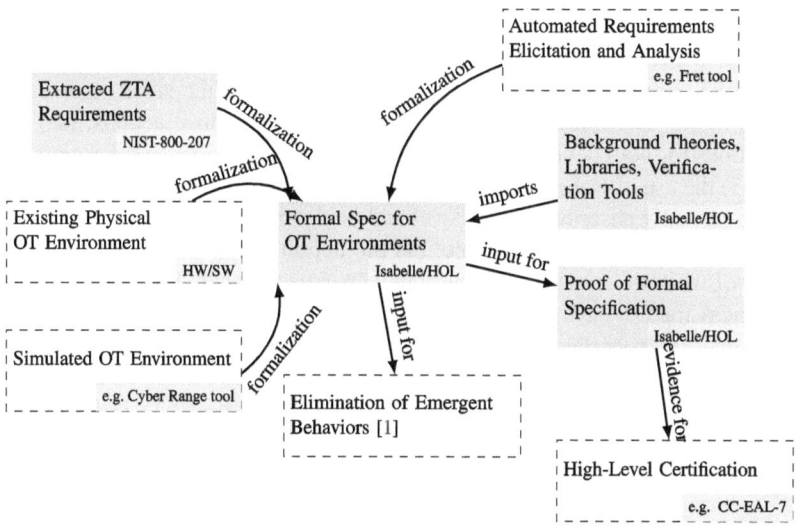

Fig. 1. Formal verification framework for OT security.

The goal of this work is to demonstrate the feasibility of developing dependably secure OT environments to the level of trustworthiness required by ZTA. Our solution consists of defining and proving correctness for OT environments under requirements imposed by ZTA. This requires a formal specification of the core functionalities of OT environments, a formal specification of ZTA tenets, and a semantics framework enforcing rigorous and modular reasoning, which allows the verification of ZTA tenets for individual devices and then the composition of the verification results for the broader OT environment. The seven tenets of ZTA that we adopt are described informally using natural language in the National Institute of Standards and Technology (NIST) Special Publication 800-207 [44], in which each tenet addresses a specific security requirement.

For example, the second tenet requires the implementation of access control policies to preserve data integrity and confidentiality, regardless of the physical location of the client accessing the network of the OT environment.

Vision. Our vision, illustrated in Fig. 1, is to create a back end for system-level formal verification of ZTA requirements in OT environments. The colored boxes are contributions described within this paper, and the white dashed boxes are use cases for future work. We use the interactive theorem proving (ITP) environment Isabelle/HOL [37] to define an array of formal verification tools, background theories, and libraries, that we leverage to specify and verify behaviors and security properties of OT environments at the system level. The workflow starts by manually extracting ZTA requirements (in natural language) from NIST 800-207. We then determine the core functionalities of OT environments to be formalized and verified together with the extracted requirements.

Contributions. The main contribution of this paper is a methodology for system-level formal verification of ZTA requirements in OT environments (Sect. 2). The application of our methodology to OT environments (see Sect. 3 for details on the microgrid configuration we are using as a case study) leads to our second contribution, a formal framework with the following results: (1) the extraction of a set of security functional requirements (SFRs) (e.g., see **SFR** 1 in Sect. 3) for microgrids based on ZTA tenets listed in NIST 800-207; (2) the use of Isabelle/HOL to define small-step semantics (see Subsect. 4.5 and Table 1), which formally describe control actions, i.e., critical control actions for both device-level and system-level interactions in microgrid configurations; (3) the use of Isabelle/HOL to define big-step semantics (see Subsect. 4.7 and Table 2) to formally describe system-level and device-level behaviors, e.g., the behavior of the OT environment as a whole; (4) the definition of data models to describe properties of the state space of OT environments (see Subsect. 4.2); (5) the definition of correctness for OT environments (see Subsect. 5.2); (6) the formalization of ZTA tenets as security properties on top of Isabelle/HOL (see Subsect. 4.6); (7) machine-checked proofs, including the proofs of the well-formedness conditions and the proofs of the state invariant for each individual device; and (8) machine-checked proofs of the security properties that provide assurance evidence that the OT environment meets the security objectives of ZTA.

2 Approaching OT Security with ZTA and Deductive Proofs

Approach. Figure 2 describes our three-step approach. Step (1) is manual extraction of extraction of SFRs (e.g., **SFR** 1) from ZTA tenets defined in NIST-800-207, the report in which ZTA standards are specified in natural language. Because the content of NIST-800-207 is broadly defined and intended for information technology (IT) environments, this step also includes the identification of the core functionalities of the core functionalities of the environment (system-level requirements for verifiable ZTA in microgrids). The extraction of SFRs involved collaborations with subject matter experts in power systems engineering, systems security engineering, and formal methods engineering[1]. The same requirement elicitation process led to the choice of a system architecture inspired by the *Enclave Gateway Model* in the same NIST-800-207 standard

---

[1] All these roles are fulfilled by the authors of this paper.

(see Fig. 3b) as an architecture model for verifiable ZTA in microgrid configurations. The main output from step (1) is a collection of SFRs for the security of microgrids that comply with ZTA; an example of SFRs are **SFR** 1 defined in Sect. 3. Once the SFRs are defined, we then extract two artifacts. The first artifact consists of system-level requirements (functional requirements), i.e., the core functionalities of OT environments that allow us to implement a secure microgrid following the architecture of the Enclave Gateway Model (see Sect. 3, Sect. 2-6). The second artifact is a list of ZTA security objectives for microgrids.

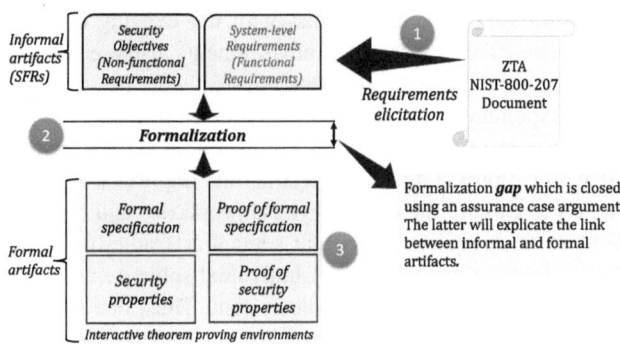

Fig. 2. Approaching OT security with verification based on deductive proofs.

Step (2) is *formalization* (see Fig. 2), i.e., translation of informal artifacts (e.g., the extracted SFRs which are written in natural language) to formal artifacts (e.g., SFRs written as a statement in logic) to allow verification via deductive proofs. This formalization step is important because it removes any ambiguity, inconsistency, incompleteness, and errant reasoning from the SFRs. In this paper, the formalization of SFRs is done manually. A manual formalization process could lead to a non-correspondence between the informal and formal artifacts, i.e., the traceability link between informal artifacts and formal artifacts might not be accurate nor complete. To resolve this issue, we develop an assurance case argument similar to those in [13, 18, 36] to justify the gap (see Fig. 2, step 2) created by a manual formalization step.

The output artifacts from the formalization step are: (a) the behavioral specification, namely, a formal specification of the core functionalities of microgrids (e.g., the closed-loop controller **WholeMG** formalized in Subsect. 4.7), well-formedness conditions, and state invariants (e.g., the state invariant **ECurrentCBrkr_inv** formalized in Subsect. 4.6), i.e., an embedding of the functional requirements in the logic of Isabelle/HOL; and, (b) security properties for microgrid configurations (e.g., the SFR **RTU_SFR** formalized in Subsect. 4.6), i.e., an embedding of the security objectives in the logic of Isabelle/HOL.

Step (3) is to use Isabelle/HOL to generate machine checked deductive proofs for the formal specification; these deductive proofs are our evidential artifacts supporting the security claim stating that "The OT environment is secure following ZTA". This includes proving that the behavioral specification of a given microgrid configuration preserves the state invariant, the well-formedness conditions, and the security properties.

Main Challenges. The main challenges of our approach are related to the formal verification of OT environments, such as system complexity (e.g., the system of systems nature of OT environments) and maintenance (e.g., continuous deployment). Given the ongoing transition to renewable energy, OT environments are under continuous deployment (i.e., frequently updated and maintained) in which heterogeneous devices, which have individual control actions and are implemented separately, are integrated to operate together using asynchronous communication protocols. Continuous deployment connects new, small configurations (subsystems) with the existing configuration of the broader OT environment. The design of OT environments also creates a cyber-physical environment mixing continuous behaviors (the physical side, i.e., the controller infrastructure and its corresponding control actions) and discrete behaviors (the cyber side, i.e., the communication infrastructure and its corresponding control actions). From the point of view of verification via deductive proofs, this requires a heterogeneous state-space representation to capture the cyber-physical properties and behaviors of the different subsystems. It also requires a modular semantics framework that allows us to describe and to reason about the behavior of individual subsystems (e.g., ICS devices) and then to compose the results for the whole system. Thus, one can expose the verification results obtained at the subsystem-level (or device-level) to system-level interactions. These challenges are severe barriers for the formal verification of OT environments, and we provide novel solutions in what follows.

Solutions. Modular formal verification of CPSs, such as OT environments that are under continuous deployment, is a significant challenge for state-of-the-art formal methods due to the reasons described above. Our solution is to use Isabelle/UTP [15] as a semantics framework to carry out the overall verification. This choice is motivated by multiple factors. First, Isabelle/UTP builds on the seminal work of Hoare & He, which uses unifying theories of programming (UTP) [21]. The latter offers an extensible framework and uses alphabetized relational calculus as a semantic foundation for the unification of features of CPSs. For example, one can incrementally extend UTP with semantics for hybrid programs [12], probabilistic programs [58], imperative programs with exceptions, heaps, and stacks, and also methods of handling the subtleties of concurrent [6,14], parallel [54], and real-time executions [9]. UTP is thus suitable for the formal verification of any OT environment (or system of systems) under continuous deployment. This is because UTP is an extensible verification framework that allows us to semantically describe and incrementally integrate verified features for CPSs. Additionally, Isabelle/UTP has a generic state-space representation using lenses [16], allowing us to describe heterogeneous state spaces, and thus mixed-discrete and continuous (hybrid) behaviors [18] of CPSs can be modeled and verified. Finally, Isabelle/UTP is based on Isabelle/HOL, and thus we will benefit from sophisticated proof engineering tools, such as: (1) parallel proof-checking [3]; (2) proof tactic customization via Eisbach [34], a large collection of libraries for the implementation of domain-specific formal languages [36,47,51,52]; and, (3) sophisticated provers and constraint solvers [10].

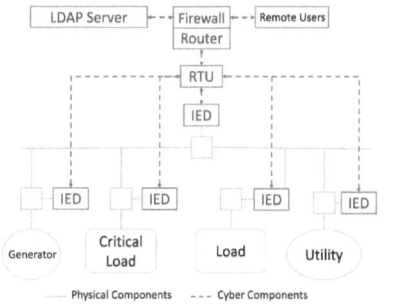
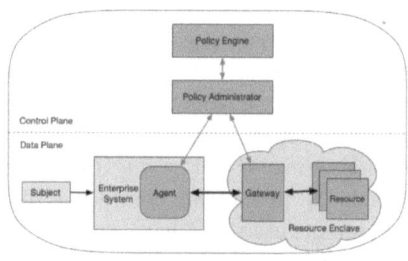

(a) A microgrid configuration (our case study)   (b) Enclave Gateway Model [44, Figure 4]

Fig. 3. Figure 3 a is inspired by Fig. 3b, where components of Fig. 3b are instantiated with ICS devices. (Color figure online)

This paper develops multiple extensions to Isabelle/UTP. First, we present a small-step semantics to describe device-level control actions (mostly cyber and a few physical) in microgrid configurations. Next, we develop a big-step semantics to compose device-level and system-level control actions, so one can describe the overall behavior of a microgrid. A distinguishing feature of our big-step semantics is the **MODIFY** operator (see Table 2), which is used to express *dynamic frames* [24,25]. This allows us to reason about independent regions of the state space in a modular way, i.e., to carry verified properties through independent regions of the state space (subsystems of the OT environment under verification) and compose them with properties of other independent regions to form a larger state space inheriting the verified properties for free. Then, we develop an extended rule set for Hoare logic to reason about the small-step and big-step semantics in a syntax-directed way. Our *dynamic frame rule* (introduced in Subsect. 5.3) for the **MODIFY** operator is a novel contribution that allows for modular reasoning with Hoare logic. Finally, we developed a modular and dynamic verification condition generator (VCG), which uses our extended rule set for Hoare logic to automatically generate verification conditions. The novelty for our VCG is the automated usage of the dynamic frame rule to discharge an already proven statement about properties of smaller regions of the state space (subsystems) when composed with larger regions.

3   Case Study: A Microgrid Configuration for the Control of DERs

To demonstrate the applicability of our approach presented in Sect. 2, we use the OT environment depicted in Fig. 3a, a microgrid configuration for the control of a set of DERs. The microgrid consists of a generator, a critical load, a noncritical load, utility, and breakers (denoted by orange squares) as physical components. The configuration also integrates devices such as IEDs, RTUs, router, firewall, and an LDAP server as the cyber components. The orange solid line (physical) represents the power line, i.e., where the electric current is transported. The blue dashed line (cyber) is the distributed control network infrastructure (the communication network). This paper focuses on the formal verification of the devices (in blue) and the system-level interactions between them (blue dashed line). The verification of the physical components is out of scope of this work.

Figure 3a is a security architecture inspired by Fig. 3b, where components of Fig. 3b are instantiated by ICS devices in Fig. 3a. For example, IEDs and RTU are the main critical resources we would like to protect (our *Resource Enclave*). The firewall and router are our *Gateway* securing access to the critical resources. The LDAP server is the *Policy Administrator* and *Engine* implementing the access control policy. The *Agent* is not considered; instead, we consider the *System* (i.e., web portal) through which *subjects* (i.e., remote users) can have a remote access to the Resource Enclave.

In this microgrid configuration, the role of the IEDs is to read and then process sensor data following the implemented control logic at the device level. In Fig. 3a, the main functionality of IEDs is to issue control commands to actuate (i.e., open or close) its assigned circuit breaker. IEDs are critical components because their control commands can badly affect the underlying DERs. For example, if the IED randomly open and close the breakers, then the generator can incur damages [53] that range from an electrical outage for a short period of time to a more safety-critical event, such as a long-term outage (e.g., Florida 2008 outage shutdown[2]). Given their critical role in microgrid configurations, and because IEDs can directly connect to the network and have system-level interactions with other devices (e.g., an RTU), it is essential to formally verify that these devices are secure following ZTA requirements, and thus avoiding scenarios with bad outcomes.

Similarly, the RTU is another critical resource we aim to prove to be secure because of its critical role in microgrid configurations. The role of the RTU is to act as a SCADA that receives the data from IEDs. Based on the collected data, the RTU can send requests to IEDs to either open or close the circuit breakers. The data collected by the RTU are usually sent to other devices for analysis and to determine the current condition of the microgrid. Because RTUs are devices that can be accessed remotely, and because they can control other critical devices (i.e., IEDs) and store critical data, we formally verify that access to these devices is secure, and that their system-level interactions do not lead to an inconsistent state of the microgrid configuration.

The LDAP server has the role of policy administrator and engine in the microgrid configuration depicted in Fig. 3a. The LDAP server is an application protocol for accessing and maintaining distributed directory information services over an Internet Protocol (IP) network. Directory services play an important role in developing intranet and Internet applications by allowing the sharing of information about users, systems, networks, services, and applications throughout the network. For examples, directory services can provide any organized set of records, often with a hierarchical structure, such as a corporate email directory. All the usernames, passwords, and their corresponding authorization attributes are stored in the LDAP server. LDAP servers are responsible for the authentication and authorization of access of user clients to each device.

Finally, the firewall and router in Fig. 3a represent the security gateway. The router forwards the network packets to the desired devices based on their IP addresses. The firewall monitors the incoming and outgoing network packets and determines whether

---

[2] https://www.icscybersecurityconference.com/demo-hacking-protective-relay-taking-control-grid-risk/.

the packet need to be transmitted or dropped based on the previously configured set of rules. The network packets can be filtered according to the source and destination IP addresses, protocol, source and destination ports, and encryption state. The filtering in our system is based on IP addresses, ports, and protocol.

To formally verify that the microgrid configuration depicted in Fig. 3a is secure, and that its behavior is functionally correct as required by NIST 800-207, we follow the 3 steps captured in Fig. 2 and explained in Sect. 2. The first step is to translate ZTA tenets to SFRs (i.e., implementations of ZTA tenets with components of microgrids). For example, the following SFR is manually extracted from ZTA tenet number 2:

SFR 1. *If the microgrid configuration depicted in Fig. 3a is in a consistent state, then a user can have remote access to any of the devices in the microgrid through web portal login by the following steps. i) Server authentication: If a user wants to log into any of the devices, first, the user should verify the server certificate to authenticate the server. In this microgrid configuration, this is internally achieved by the use of Transport Layer Security (TLS) protocol [40]. ii) User Authentication: Once the encrypted channel is established, the user must be authenticated to perform any actions related to the device, such as changing settings/configurations and issuing commands. The user authentication is performed after the user enters a username and password. This information is sent to the LDAP server, and the LDAP server checks the database and issues an authentication for the user if the credentials are valid. iii) User Authorization: User authorization is based on user credentials. The LDAP server checks its database and issues the authorization attributes, such as privilege level, to the user, and this information is propagated to devices. The steps (i)-(iii) should not lead to inconsistent states of the microgrid configuration.*

The formal specification presented in Sect. 4 and verified in Sect. 5 is centered around this SFR. This SFR directly responds to the ZTA Tenet 2 in NIST 800-207 because it prevents cyber threats, such as man-in-the-middle attacks and server spoofing. Other SFRs were defined to address this and other ZTA tenets (the relation between ZTA tenets and SFRs can be one-to-many), but it will not be presented here for brevity.

4 Formal Modeling of Microgrids

This section presents a formal specification for the microgrid configuration described in Fig. 3a. Our goal is to verify **SFR** 1 introduced in Sect. 3. The formal specification is composed of: (1) models to describe the state space of the microgrid (see Subsect. 4.2, Subsect. 4.3, and Subsect. 4.4); (2) state invariants and enabling conditions to describe the consistency of the microgrid configuration (see Subsect. 4.6); (3) a small-step semantics to describe single stage operations (see Subsect. 4.5); (4) a big-step semantics to compose these operations and model the behavior of devices and the behavior of the system as whole (see Subsect. 4.7); and (5) automated and modular proofs of the desired properties (see Subsect. 5.2 and Subsect. 5.3). In Subsect. 4.1 we will introduce preliminaries on Isabelle/HOL which is the formal specification language we are using.

4.1   Notations

The notation used in this paper assumes familiarity with higher order logic (HOL) and its implementation in the ITP Isabelle/HOL [37]. Isabelle/HOL is a proof assistant that has features of functional programming languages and includes a support for HOL specifications and structured interactive proofs. The $\land$, $\lor$, $\forall$, and $\exists$ are the usual logical connectors for Boolean expressions. Notations for set theory—such as $\cap$, $\cup$, and $\{\}$— are also supported. The term language of Isabelle/HOL has a lambda calculus abstract syntax. For example, a non-recursive function has the following notation:

```
definition add1 x = x + 1
```

... where **add1** is the name of the function, x is the input argument, and $x + 1$ is the "return" value (the image of x). The same function can have an equivalent notation using a lambda-like abstract syntax, as follows: $\lambda x \ . \ x + 1$. Functional programming features such as **let** expressions, well-founded recursive functions via **fun**, syntax trees via **datatype** (which can also be used as an enumeration type), primitive-type definitions via **typedef**, and records-type definitions via **record** (tuples with an advanced infrastructure improving proof automation) are also supported by the term language of Isabelle/HOL. Boolean terms that require interactive proofs are specified using:

```
lemma inter_is_idempotent:
  "A ∩ A = A"
by auto
```

... where `inter_is_idempotent` is an optional label name for the theorem to be proven, `"A ∩ A = A"` is the theorem specifying the algebraic property, and **by** auto is the proof of the theorem; in this case, the proof was automatically generated using the proof tactic auto. Structured and human-readable proofs are also supported using the proof language Isabelle/Isar [50]. We believe that this brief introduction to Isabelle's term language reviews the frequently used terms and symbols, so the rest of this paper will make free use of Isabelle notation.

4.2   Data Models

The data models used for the specification of the state space of the microgrid configuration described in Fig. 3a is bifurcated into the state space for each individual device (e.g., state space model of IED devices described in Subsect. 4.3) and the state space for the whole system (introduced in Subsect. 4.4). The data model describing the state space for individual devices is an abstraction of CONFIG files used by real world ICS devices. In our model, each individual device is seen as a CONFIG file which has a logic module and communications module. For example, the model for basic data used to specify components of CONFIG files used by IEDs is defined in Isabelle/HOL as follows:

```
type_synonym ECURRENT = int
type_synonym TIME = nat -- {*Time unit*}
type_synonym ID=nat--{*Identification #*}
type_synonym CBRKRID = ID
```

```
type_synonym IEDID = ID
datatype CBRKRSTATUS = cOpen  | cClosed
datatype ALARM = silent | alarming
datatype IEDSTATUS =
  iedOperational | gotCmdRTU |iedShutdown|
  . . .
```

... in which types fully written with upper cases are either type synonyms of Isabelle's primitive types (specified using **type_synonym**) or enumeration types (specified using **datatype**). For example, the **type_synonym** ECURRENT denotes electrical current, and it is specified using Isabelle's primitive type for signed integers int. We use signed integers to model the direction of the electrical current flow. For example, in +5, the sign + means that the electrical current flows away from the device, and the value 5 is the magnitude of current (in Amperes).

4.3   State Space of ICS Devices in Isabelle/UTP

The state space of ICS devices that are components of the microgrid under verification is specified using **alphabet**, which is used by Isabelle/UTP to mimic Isabelle/HOL record types. The main difference between Isabelle/HOL record types specified using **record** and Isabelle/UTP types that are specified using **alphabet** is that the fields of **alphabet** are lenses [16] (i.e., an algebraic structure used to describe variables in an axiomatic way). We have contributed a new version for the **alphabet** package allowing for type overloading. For example, the Isabelle/UTP representation of the state space of IEDs is specified using a record of lenses as follows:

```
alphabet IEDCyberInter =        alphabet IED =
  status       :: IEDSTATUS       ied_id       :: IEDID
  rtuCmdTimeout:: TIME            iedCyberInter:: IEDCyberInter
alphabet CBrkrECurrent =         eCurrentCBrkr:: CBrkrECurrent
  cBrkrID        :: CBRKRID
  cBrkrStatus    :: CBRKRSTATUS
  currentECurrent:: ECURRENT
  . . .
```

... where each field of record types specified using **alphabet** models an independent region of the state space. For example, the root type IED is a record with three fields. The first field of IED is the lens ied_id, which has the view type IEDID, and models the identification number of the device. As a result, the lens ied_id will use a value from the type IEDID to store the identification number of a given IED The second field of the record type IED is iedCyberInter, a lens that characterizes a region of the state space independent from the one characterized by the lens ied_id. The lens iedCyberInter stores information related to cyber interactions between an IED and other devices, such as RTU. The lens iedCyberInter has the view type IEDCyberInter, specifying a record of lenses, and it includes the field status which uses the type IEDSTATUS to store the status of the IED when interacting with its assigned RTU (see Fig. 3a). The field `rtuCmdTimeout` of the record type `IEDCyberInter` stores the time-out thresh-old for responding to requests sent by the RTU. The third field of the record type `IED` is the lens `eCurrentCBrkr`, which characterizes another independent region of the state space, and it is used to store information about the physical components inter-acting with IED. In this case, the lens `eCurrentCBrkr` will store information related to the circuit breaker that is controlled by the IED. The lens `eCurrentCBrkr` has the view type `CBrkrECurrent`, specifying a record of lenses, in which each lens stores information related to the circuit breaker controlled by the IED. For example, the lens `cBrkrStatus` of the record type `CBrkrECurrent` is used to model the status of the circuit breaker. The lens `cBrkrStatus` has the view type `CBRKRSTATUS`, which allows the status of the breaker to take one of two values: `cOpen`, when it is open; or `cClosed`, when it is closed. Similarly, we model the state spaces of the other devices, such as the RTU, the LDAP server, the firewall, and the router.

4.4   State Space of the Whole Microgrid

The data model describing the state space of the whole microgrid (described in Fig. 3a) is used to additionally capture the effects of system-level interactions (i.e., signals sent between devices). The Isabelle/UTP model for the state space of the system as a whole is defined as follows:

```
alphabet ControlledVars =          alphabet Devices =
  cBrkrCon   :: CBRKRSTATUS          ied :: IEDID => IED option
  . . .                              rtu :: RTU
alphabet MonitoredVars =            . . .
  eCurrentMon    :: ECURRENT        alphabet MGConfig =
  maxECurrentMon:: ECURRENT           devices:: Devices
alphabet Environment =              env    :: Environment
  controlled:: ControlledVars
  monitored :: MonitoredVars
```

...in which the root record has the type `MGConfig`, and specifies the whole microgrid configuration. The field `devices` of the lens record `MGConfig` has the type `Devices`, which is itself a record of lenses. It is used to model the state space of devices that are components of the microgrid configuration. The field `env` of the lens record `MGConfig` has the type `Environment`, and it is used to model the state space of the physical environment.

The modeling pattern used to describe the state space of the physical environment is similar to the one used in [2, 18, 36]. The pattern splits the physical environment into: monitored variables (sensors) and controlled variables (actuators). Monitored variables store the sensed data from the outside environment (e.g., sensing the value of the electri-cal current, which is modeled by the lens `eCurrentMon`), and the controlled variables store the status of the physical components that can be changed by devices, e.g., the IED can actuate (i.e., open and close) the circuit breaker, which is modeled by the lens `cBrkrCon`.

Table 1. Syntax and description of the small-step semantics (selected list).

Constructs	Description
`UserLogOnToRTU`	This is a multistage operation. This operation can be instantiated for any device allowing remote access through the web portal (in this case, the RTU) It represents a state-transition system where each transition is a single-stage operation that represents a step that is required to log on to the device The transitions are mainly related to authentication and authorization operations which model the steps of the TLS protocol
`IEDOpenBreaker`	This is a single-stage operation. This operation can be executed by IEDs. The main effect of this operation is to open the breaker
`IEDCloseBreaker`	The effect is to close the breaker. Otherwise, same as `IEDOpenBreaker`
`RTUSendLDAPAuthCheckRequest`	The RTU sends a signal to the RTU server to check if the user has the access rights to log on to this RTU
`RTURecvLDAPAuthCheckRequestOK`	RTU receives a signal from the LDAP that the user access request is accepted
`RTURecvLDAPAuthCheckRequestFail`	RTU receives a signal from the LDAP that the user access request is denied

4.5 Small-Step Semantics

The system-level view of the microgrid configuration depicted in Fig. 3a consists of a composition of single-stage operations performed by devices to update their own state space and also single-stage operations to interact with other devices and update the state space of the whole microgrid. We call these single-stage operations the small-step semantics. A general representation for these single-stage operations in Isabelle/HOL is:

`op` $= \lambda$ `s s'.` **E**`(s)` $\longrightarrow$ **A**`(s,s')`

... where **op** can be substituted by any operation from Table 1, and **E**(s) is a Boolean expression, i.e., it is a unary relation (a predicate) on the initial state s. **E**(s) specifies the enabling condition for the single-stage operation **op**. **A**(s, s') is a binary relation between the initial state s and the final state s'. **A**(s, s') specifies the effect of the operation on the state space, i.e., substitutions of the values of variables (lenses) at state s with new values that yield a new state s'.

In fact, enabling conditions, **E**(s), are guards for single-stage operations. That is if **E**(s) is evaluated to be true, then the behavior of **op** is characterized by the set of reachable states denoted by the relation **A**(s, s'). If **E**(s) is false, however, then the behavior of **op** is completely nondeterministic, i.e., **op** will have a divergent set of reachable states and will behave exactly as **DIVERGE** from Table 2. At the implementation level, enabling conditions are used to describe constraints on a particular region of the state space, such as time constraints that a given variable should satisfy or constraints about the range of possible values for a given variable. For example, the single-stage operation **IEDOpenBreaker** from Table 1, which is performed by IED, has the following semantics in Isabelle/HOL:

```
definition IEDOpenBrkr eCurrentValue =
λ s s'.
 abs (lens_lookup maxECurrent (s)) ≤ abs (eCurrentValue) ⟶
 s' = lens_upd cBrkrStatus s (cOpen)
```

... where **E**(s) is substituted by the Boolean expression:

abs (lens_lookup maxECurrent (s)) $\leq$ abs (eCurrentValue)

...and **A**(s,s') is substituted by s' = lens_upd cBrkrStatus s (cOpen). The input argument eCurrentValue represents the electrical current that the IED senses from the power line. maxECurrent is a lens characterizing a region of the state space where the maximum value of the electrical current is stored. abs is a function that returns the absolute value of a signed integer. lens_lookup is a function that retrieves the value of a given lens at a specified state; in this case, it was used to retrieve the value of the maximum current stored in maxECurrent. For simplicity, we will use the notation X!!s instead of lens_lookup X (s). cBrkrStatus is a lens storing the status of the circuit breaker (described in Subsect. 4.2). lens_upd is a function that updates a lens with a given value at a given state; in this case, it was used to update cBrkrStatus with the value cOpen. The full definition of **IEDOpenBrkr** has additional input arguments and performs more substitutions on the state s. Details are omitted here for brevity.

4.6   Invariants and Security Properties

We use state invariants to specify the consistency of the microgrid. A state invariant is a predicate on the state, s, that specifies a consistent state for a given device and for the microgrid as a whole. To prove that the state invariant is preserved by the microgrid configuration, we assume that the invariant holds on the initial state, and we prove that it still holds after performing any microgrid's operation. For the case of circuit breakers controlled by IEDs, the state invariant has the following notation in Isabelle/HOL:

definition ECurrentCBrkr_inv s =
(abs (maxECurrent!!s) >
 abs (currentECurrent!!s) $\longleftrightarrow$ ((cBrkrStatus!!s) = cClosed $\wedge$
    ...) $\wedge$
((eCurrentAlarm !!s) = alarming $\longleftrightarrow$
 ((cBrkrStatus !!s) = cClosed $\wedge$ (currentTime!!s) $\geq$ (
    alarmTimeout!!s)$\wedge$ ...))

...Here, the invariant is a conjunction of cases specifying a consistent state of the circuit breaker. This specifies the consistent state of the variables cBrkrStatus and eCurrentAlarm. The invariant **ECurrentCBrkr_inv** has the following specification pattern:

case1 $\wedge$ case2 $\wedge$ ...

...where each case has the following pattern:

 Z(s) $\longleftrightarrow$ P(s) $\wedge$ Q(s) $\wedge$ ...

For example, the case:

(eCurrentAlarm!!s)=alarming $\longleftrightarrow$ (cBrkrStatus !!s)=cClosed $\wedge$...

is the case where the invariant **ECurrentCBrkr_inv** specifies when the alarm should be alarming. Other state invariants that specify the consistency of the other devices are formalized, but are omitted here for brevity.

Similarly, we formalize **SFR** 1 from Sect. 3 as a security property for the RTU in the form of a predicate on the state. The reason we do not instantiate **SFR** 1 for IEDs is because we assume that user access to IEDs is possible only through a web portal log-in to RTU. Specifically, we assume that no direct access to IEDs is possible for remote users without admin privileges. To prove that the security property **RTU_SFR** defined below is satisfied, we assume it to be true on the initial state of the microgrid and then prove it to be true after the execution of the microgrid's operations.

```
definition RTU_SFR cportID usrID t s =
((rtuSrvrStatus!!s) = rtuOperational ∧
 RTU_inv_1_10 cportID usrID t s ∧
 ValidLDAPServer (rtuCurrentLDAP!!s) ∧
 ValidDigiCertificate t (rtuDigiCert!!s) ∧
 (∃ c. c = (rtuDigiCert!!s) ∧
  ValidKeyStore t c (rtuKeyStore!!s)) ∧
 (∀ s'. s ∈ {s.
  (rtuSrvrStatus cportID usrID t s) = rtu_UserLogOn ∧
   UserLogOnToRTU cportID usrID t s s'} ⟶
 UCWithRTUCADC cportID usrID t s ∧
 UCAuthCheckSuccess cportID usrID t s ∧
 UCLDAPCredSuccess cportID usrID t s))
```

RTU_SFR, described above, is a formalization of **SFR** 1 from Sect. 3 instantiated for the RTU device. rtuOperational means that the RTU is not administrated by an admin, and it is in a state of waiting for log-in requests from a remote user, usrID, through the web portal, cportID. The input arguments t and s specifies the current time and the current state of the microgrid, respectively. **RTU_inv_1_10** is an Isabelle **definition** that specifies the state invariant of the RTU, i.e., the consistent state of the RTU. As explained in Sect. 3, because **SFR** 1 is enforcing authentication and authorization via the TLS protocol and the LDAP server, we use **ValidLDAPServer** to specify the consistency of the LDAP server. For example, **ValidLDAPServer** allows us to check the consistency of the LDAP server after its enrollment by an administrator. For the same reason, we use **ValidDigiCertificate** to specify the validity of the digital certificate. Both **ValidLDAPServer** and **ValidDigiCertificate** are Isabelle **definition**s, and the details of their specifications are omitted for brevity. The rest of the specification of **RTU_SFR**, starting from ∀s'. s ∈ {s. ...} ⟶ ... until the end, describes the set of states that lead to rtu_UserLogOn by executing the multistage operation **UserLogOnToRTU** while satisfying the following:

- **UCWithRTUCADC**, which specifies that the server authentication was successful, i.e., the user client authenticated the digital certificate of the RTU.
- **UCLDAPCredSuccess**, which specifies that the user authentication was successful, i.e., the RTU authenticated the credentials of the user client. This check is done by the LDAP server.
- **UCAuthCheckSuccess**, which specifies that the user client is authorized to log into the RTU with its assigned privileges.

Table 2. Syntax and description of the big-step semantics.

Constructs	Description
SKIP	Used to semantically capture stutter states;
	(e.g., to model a non-terminating loop, one can use SKIP as a single statement
	for the body of the while-loop and keep the loop-condition true).
MAGIC	The program that has an empty set of reachable states. Known as the perfect program.
	It is perfect because it refines any specification. Namely, the Hoare triple {P}MAGIC{Q}
	is proven to be true for any assumption P and any guarantee Q! We are using this program
	to make properties of the other constructs semantically visible.
DIVERGE	The program that has a divergent set of reachable states. The worst program!
X :== e	Basic assignment of the value of an expression e to a region of the state space
	characterized by the lens X.
P ;; Q	Sequentially execute the program P then Q; this is used to sequentially compose statements.
μ R• P	Least fixed point (LFP). Used to model recursion of program P with R occurring in P
	and representing the point where the recursion is unfolded.
Conditional	Notation: IF b THEN P ELSE Q FI; It means execute P if b, else execute Q.
Nondeterminism	Notation: P ⊓ Q. It means the union between the set of states that are reachable by
	the program P and the set of states that are reachable by the program Q.
Iterations	Notation: FROM P UNTIL b DO Q OD. It means execute P one time, then repeatedly
	execute Q until b becomes true. Can be modelled with a combination of sequential composition
	construct, and conditional statement, and the recursion construct as follows:
	P ;; (μ R• IF¬ b THEN Q ;; R ELSE SKIP FI).
Framing	Notation: MODIFY X DO P OD. It means execute the program P and discard all changes
	made by P outside the region of the state space (the frame) characterized by the lens X.

4.7 Big-Step Semantics

The behavior of the system as a whole is modeled using the closed-loop controller defined by **WholeMG** below. Input arguments (parameters) of **WholeMG** are omitted here for simplicity. **WholeMG** uses big-step semantics constructs from Table 2 to compose single-stage operations from Table 1 and define the behavior of the microgrid as a whole.

```
definition WholeMG =
   FROM init s s' until False
      DO SensingEnv  s s';; ChangingEnv s s';;
         DiscreteControl s s';; ContinuousDynamics s s' OD
```

WholeMG performs a sequence of controls, each of which changes a region of the state space of the whole microgrid (the state space of the microgrid as a whole is specified using the record of lenses MGConfig in Subsect. 4.4). In **WholeMG**, the system-level behavior **SensingEnv** will update the state space of each device by the value of the corresponding monitored variable (i.e., the behavior **SensingEnv** reads values from regions of the record of lenses MonitoredVars specified in Subsect. 4.4). For example, an IED will periodically sense the magnitude and the direction of the current from the power line. The sensed value is stored in the monitored variable (lens) eCurrentMon.

The system-level behavior **ChangingEnv** specifies periodic updates on controlled variables from the physical environment (the state space of the physical environment is specified using the record of lenses Environment, which is in Subsect. 4.4). For example, an IED can actuate the physical circuit breaker to change its status. The physical status of the circuit breaker is modeled by the controlled variable (lens) cBrkrCon. The system-level behavior **DiscreteControl** specifies all possible cyber controls that can be performed by devices belonging to the microgrid configuration. For example, a possible behavior for **DiscreteControl** is the multistage operation **UserLogOnToRTU** from Table 1. Finally, **ContinuousDynamics** specifies the periodic updates that are done by the environment on the monitored variables. For example, we allow the environment to assign random values for the monitored variable eCurrentMon.

5   Formal Verification of Microgrids

5.1   Modular Verification Approach

Modular verification is a significant challenge when using formal methods. Because a microgrid configuration is a system of systems that is under continuous deployment, it requires a modular verification approach. To enable modular verification for the behavior of microgrids, we use the framing operator **MODIFY** from Table 2. The framing operator allows us to lift the verification results obtained at the level of single-stage operations to the device level and then to the system level. Specifically, the framing operator will allow us to carry through the verified properties on a given region of the state space (the frame) using the lens characterizing that region. For example, we prove that the single-stage operation **IEDOpenBrkr**, which we formally defined in Subsect. 4.5, maintains the invariant **ECurrentCBrkr_inv** (which is defined in Subsect. 4.6), then we use the framing operator to lift the operation **IEDOpenBrkr** to the device level using **IEDOpenBrkr_dvc** defined below.

```
definition IEDOpenBrkr_dvc =
MODIFY eCurrentCBrkr DO IEDOpenBrkr OD
```

IEDOpenBrkr_dvc is a lifting that enables the use of the frame rule (see Subsect. 5.3), which carries the verified properties about the operation **IEDOpenBrkr** through to the device level using the lens eCurrentCBrkr. Similarly, we lift the device level behavior **IEDOpenBrkr_dvc** to the system level, which allows us to use the frame rule again to carry the verified properties about **IEDOpenBrkr_dvc** through to the system level using the lens devices:

```
definition IEDOps_sys =
MODIFY devices DO IEDOpenBrkr_dvc ⊓ IEDCloseBrkr_dvc OD
```

where **IEDOps_sys** describes the system-level behavior for IEDs, which is one possible behavior for **DiscreteControl**. The latter is the discrete (cyber) part of the cyber-physical behavior of the closed-loop controller **WholeMG** described in Subsect. 4.7.

5.2   Correctness for Microgrids

The goal of this work is to expose single-stage operations to system-level interactions and ensure that the security properties and invariants (e.g., see Subsect. 4.6) still hold. To prove correctness for the microgrid configuration depicted in Fig. 3a, we first prove that the closed-loop controller **WholeMG** that we introduced in Subsect. 4.7 preserves the state invariants (e.g., system-level interactions don't break the state invariant **ECurrentCBrkr_inv** from Subsect. 4.6). Then, we prove that **WholeMG** preserves the **SFR** 1 that we described in natural language in Sect. 3 and then formalized in Isabelle/HOL in Subsect. 4.6 using the definition **RTU_SFR**. To do such proofs, we employ Hoare logic and VCG-based reasoning, such as in [4,30,59]. Our Hoare triple is defined in Isabelle/HOL as follows:

definition ⦃P⦄B⦃Q⦄ =
{(s,s'). P (s)} ∩ {(s,s'). B (s, s')} ⊆ {(s,s'). Q (s')}

... where P is a predicate that characterizes the set of initial states (i.e., what we assume), B is a behavior expressed using either Table 2 or any operation from Table 1 (e.g., B can be substituted by the closed-loop controller **WholeMG** from Subsect. 4.7), and Q is a predicate that characterizes the set of final states (i.e., what we guarantee), e.g., Q can be substituted by the state invariant **ECurrentCBrkr_inv** and the security property **RTU_SFR** we introduced in Subsect. 4.6. Based on this notation for the Hoare triple, we define the Hoare logic for the big-step and small-step semantics.

5.3   Frame Rule

A distinguishing feature of our Hoare logic is the generic scheme for the frame rule, which allows us to enforce modular reasoning. Our frame rule is expressed in Isabelle/HOL as follows:

lemma frame_rule:
  assume ⦃P⦄B⦃Q⦄
  shows ⦃P∧R⦄**MODIFY** X **DO** B **OD**⦃(∃Y(Q))∧(∃X(R))⦄
proof ...

This Isabelle/HOL theorem specifies our frame_rule. Intuitively, the theorem means: If a behavior, B, guarantees the property, Q, starting from the assumptions, P, then the frame operator, **MODIFY**, will use the lens, X, to carry the guarantee, Q. The guarantees of regions of the state space which are independent from X are characterized by R, and are carried through using the lens, Y. For example, Y can characterize the already-deployed regions of the state space (i.e., the existing system of systems), and X characterizes the state space of the newly deployed and integrated subsystem. This yields the ability to verify a system of systems, such as microgrids, in a modular way. Other assumptions required to prove the theorem frame_rule are omitted here for brevity.

Our implemented VCG uses this frame rule (its weakest precondition version) to automatically discharge proofs about security properties and state invariants such as those presented in Subsect. 4.6. These properties are proved to be true on single-stage operations, and the proofs are lifted to the system level using the frame rule. In contrast to the state of the art, where the frame rules are rather specific to spatial reasoning (e.g., reasoning on heaps, such as in separation logic) or temporal reasoning (see, e.g., in [59]), our frame rule is generic and can be instantiated for both spatial and temporal reasoning.

6 Related Work

While the use of integrated formal methods with assurance cases for the full specification and verification of an OT system's safety and security properties is described as a relatively new opportunity in [19], there are a few cases in the literature in which formal methods are integrated with system behavioral models and verified using theorem proving. Khan et al. develop a three-part approach to prove system reliability and security for an OT system, in which they use Coq [39] to prove that the system is secure by design, dReal to perform vulnerability analysis, and their own product, ARMET [26], to assess vulnerability to false data injection attacks in real-time, using an example of a gravity-draining water tank. In [7,33], the authors present VeriDrone, a framework to specify and verify OT systems within the Coq proof assistant; however, the authors focus their application on safety properties of the system while we focus more on security at the cyber and cyber-physical layers.

The closest work to that which we propose is the work by Foster et al. [13], in which the authors formally verify the CPS Tokeneer using Isabelle/SACM [36]. In a similar approach, Cofer et al. [8] develop a formal specification of two separate unmanned aerial vehicles, using the JKind model checker [17] to formally verify model correctness, then using the Isabelle/HOL theorem prover [37] to prove the system's security properties and that the software implementation matches the specification. The work of Cofer et al. includes the automatic generation of software using the formal specification, but unlike the work in Foster et al. , it does not include a model-based assurance case to connect less formalized factors (e.g., regulatory text) with artifacts that can be modeled using formal methods. Finally, in an industrial case study that focuses on protocols, Dreier et al. [11] formally define a metric related to secure message passing, which they term *flow integrity*, and then apply this framework to two known protocols used in ICS, OPC-UA [32] and Modbus [38].

Acknowledgment. This work was authored by the National Renewable Energy Laboratory (NREL), operated by Alliance for Sustainable Energy, LLC, for the U.S. Department of Energy (DOE) under Contract No. DE-AC36-08GO28308. This work was supported by the Laboratory Directed Research and Development (LDRD) Program at NREL. The views expressed in the article do not necessarily represent the views of the DOE or the U.S. Government. The U.S. Government retains and the publisher, by accepting the article for publication, acknowledges that the U.S. Government retains a nonexclusive, paid-up, irrevocable, worldwide license to publish or reproduce the published form of this work, or allow others to do so, for U.S. Government purposes.

References

1. Anantharaman, P., et al.: Mismorphism: the heart of the weird machine. In: Anderson, J., Stajano, F., Christianson, B., Matyáš, V. (eds.) Security Protocols 2019. LNCS, vol. 12287, pp. 113–124. Springer, Cham (2020). https://doi.org/10.1007/978-3-030-57043-9_11
2. Barnes, J., Johnson, R., Widmaier, J.C.: Engineering the Tokeneer enclave protection software. In: 1st IEEE International Symposium on Secure Software Engineering, ISSSE 2006, Proceedings (2006)

3. Barras, B., et al.: Pervasive parallelism in highly-trustable interactive theorem proving systems. In: Carette, J., Aspinall, D., Lange, C., Sojka, P., Windsteiger, W. (eds.) CICM 2013. LNCS (LNAI), vol. 7961, pp. 359–363. Springer, Heidelberg (2013). https://doi.org/10.1007/978-3-642-39320-4_29

4. Bockenek, J., Lammich, P., Nemouchi, Y., Wolff, B.: Using Isabelle/UTP for the verification of sorting algorithms. In: Proceedings of the Isabelle Workshop, FLoC 2018, Proceedings (2018)

5. Burns, A., Davis, R.: Mixed criticality systems-a review. Department of Computer Science, University of York, Technical report, pp. 1–69 (2013)

6. Butterfield, A., Mjeda, A., Noll, J.: UTP semantics for shared-state, concurrent, context-sensitive process models. In: 2016 10th International Symposium on Theoretical Aspects of Software Engineering (TASE), pp. 93–100 (2016)

7. Chan, M., Ricketts, D., Lerner, S., Malecha, G.: Formal verification of stability properties of cyber-physical systems. In: Proceedings CoqPL (2016)

8. Cofer, D., et al.: A formal approach to constructing secure air vehicle software. Computer **51**(11), 14–23 (2018)

9. Dang Van, H., Truong, H.: Modeling and specification of real-time interfaces with UTP. In: Liu, Z., Woodcock, J., Zhu, H. (eds.) Theories of Programming and Formal Methods. LNCS, vol. 8051, pp. 136–150. Springer, Heidelberg (2013). https://doi.org/10.1007/978-3-642-39698-4_9

10. Desharnais, M., Vukmirovic, P., Blanchette, J., Wenzel, M.: Seventeen provers under the hammer. In: Andronick, J., de Moura, L. (eds.) 13th International, ITP 2022, 7–10 August 2022, Haifa, Israel. LIPIcs, vol. 237, pp. 8:1–8:18. Schloss Dagstuhl - Leibniz-Zentrum für Informatik (2022)

11. Dreier, J., Puys, M., Potet, M.-L., Lafourcade, P., Roch, J.-L.: Formally verifying flow properties in industrial systems. In: SECRYPT 2017-14th International Conference on Security and Cryptography, pp. 55–66 (2017)

12. Foster, S.: Hybrid relations in Isabelle/UTP. In: Ribeiro, P., Sampaio, A. (eds.) UTP 2019. LNCS, vol. 11885, pp. 130–153. Springer, Cham (2019). https://doi.org/10.1007/978-3-030-31038-7_7

13. Foster, S., Nemouchi, Y., Gleirscher, M., Wei, R., Kelly, T.: Integration of formal proof into unified assurance cases with Isabelle/SACM. Formal Aspects Comput. **33**(6), 855–884 (2021)

14. Foster, S., Ye, K., Cavalcanti, A., Woodcock, J.: Automated verification of reactive and concurrent programs by calculation. J. Log. Algebraic Methods Program. **121**, 100681 (2021)

15. Foster, S., Zeyda, F., Nemouchi, Y., Ribeiro, P., Wolff, B.: Isabelle/UTP: mechanised theory engineering for unifying theories of programming. Arch. Formal Proofs **2019** (2019)

16. Foster, S., Zeyda, F., Woodcock, J.: Unifying heterogeneous state-spaces with lenses. In: Sampaio, A., Wang, F. (eds.) ICTAC 2016. LNCS, vol. 9965, pp. 295–314. Springer, Cham (2016). https://doi.org/10.1007/978-3-319-46750-4_17

17. Gacek, A., Backes, J., Whalen, M., Wagner, L., Ghassabani, E.: The JKIND model checker. In: Chockler, H., Weissenbacher, G. (eds.) CAV 2018. LNCS, vol. 10982, pp. 20–27. Springer, Cham (2018). https://doi.org/10.1007/978-3-319-96142-2_3

18. Gleirscher, M., Foster, S., Nemouchi, Y.: Evolution of formal model-based assurance cases for autonomous robots. In: Ölveczky, P.C., Salaün, G. (eds.) SEFM 2019. LNCS, vol. 11724, pp. 87–104. Springer, Cham (2019). https://doi.org/10.1007/978-3-030-30446-1_5

19. Gleirscher, M., Foster, S., Woodcock, J.: New opportunities for integrated formal methods. ACM Comput. Surv. (CSUR) **52**(6), 1–36 (2019)

20. Green, B., et al.: ICS testbed tetris: practical building blocks towards a cyber security resource. In: The 13th USENIX Workshop on Cyber Security Experimentation and Test (CSET 2020) (2020)

21. Hoare, C.A.R., He, J.: Unifying Theories of Programming. Prentice Hall, Englewood Cliffs (1998)
22. Humayed, A., Lin, J., Li, F., Luo, B.: Cyber-physical systems security - a survey. IEEE Internet Things J. **4**(6), 1802–1831 (2017)
23. Johnson, J., Berg, T., Anderson, B., Wright, B.: Review of electric vehicle charger cybersecurity vulnerabilities, potential impacts, and defenses. Energies **15**(11), 3931 (2022)
24. Kassios, I.T.: Dynamic frames: support for framing, dependencies and sharing without restrictions. In: Misra, J., Nipkow, T., Sekerinski, E. (eds.) FM 2006. LNCS, vol. 4085, pp. 268–283. Springer, Heidelberg (2006). https://doi.org/10.1007/11813040_19
25. Kassios, I.T.: The dynamic frames theory. Formal Aspects Comput. **23**(3), 267–288 (2011)
26. Khan, M.T., Serpanos, D., Shrobe, H.: ARMET: behavior-based secure and resilient industrial control systems. Proc. IEEE **106**(1), 129–143 (2017)
27. Kindervag, J.: Build security into your network's DNA: the zero trust network architecture. Forrester Res., 1–26 (2010)
28. Kounev, V., Tipper, D., Yavuz, A.A., Grainger, B.M., Reed, G.F.: A secure communication architecture for distributed microgrid control. IEEE Trans. Smart Grid **6**(5), 2484–2492 (2015)
29. Kulik, T.: A survey of practical formal methods for security. Formal Aspects Comput. **34**(1), 1–39 (2022)
30. Lammich, P., Wimmer, S.: IMP2 - simple program verification in Isabelle/HOL. Arch. Formal Proofs **2019** (2019)
31. Lewis, T.G.: Critical Infrastructure Protection in Homeland Security: Defending a Networked Nation. Wiley (2019)
32. Mahnke, W., Leitner, S.-H., Damm, M.: OPC Unified Architecture. Springer, Heidelberg (2009). https://doi.org/10.1007/978-3-540-68899-0
33. Malecha, G., Ricketts, D., Alvarez, M.M., Lerner, S.: Towards foundational verification of cyber-physical systems. In: 2016 Science of Security for Cyber-Physical Systems Workshop (SOSCYPS), pp. 1–5. IEEE (2016)
34. Matichuk, D., Murray, T., Wenzel, M.: Eisbach: a proof method language for Isabelle. J. Autom. Reason. **56**(3), 261–282 (2016)
35. Moness, M., Moustafa, A.M.: A survey of cyber-physical advances and challenges of wind energy conversion systems: prospects for internet of energy. IEEE Internet Things J. **3**(2), 134–145 (2015)
36. Nemouchi, Y., Foster, S., Gleirscher, M., Kelly, T.: Isabelle/SACM: computer-assisted assurance cases with integrated formal methods. In: Ahrendt, W., Tapia Tarifa, S.L. (eds.) IFM 2019. LNCS, vol. 11918, pp. 379–398. Springer, Cham (2019). https://doi.org/10.1007/978-3-030-34968-4_21
37. Nipkow, T., Wenzel, M., Paulson, L.C. (eds.): Isabelle/HOL - A Proof Assistant for Higher-Order Logic. LNCS, vol. 2283. Springer, Heidelberg (2002). https://doi.org/10.1007/3-540-45949-9
38. MODBUS Organization: MODBUS Messaging on TCP/IP Implementation Guide: v1.0b. MODBUS Organization (2006)
39. Paulin-Mohring, C.: Introduction to the Coq proof-assistant for practical software verification. In: Meyer, B., Nordio, M. (eds.) LASER 2011. LNCS, vol. 7682, pp. 45–95. Springer, Heidelberg (2012). https://doi.org/10.1007/978-3-642-35746-6_3
40. Paulson, L.C.: The inductive approach to verifying cryptographic protocols. J. Comput. Secur. **6**(1–2), 85–128 (1998)
41. Platzer, A.: Logical Analysis of Hybrid Systems: Proving Theorems for Complex Dynamics. Springer, Heidelberg (2010). https://doi.org/10.1007/978-3-642-14509-4
42. Platzer, A.: Logical Foundations of Cyber-Physical Systems. Springer, Cham (2018). https://doi.org/10.1007/978-3-319-63588-0

43. Rocchetto, M., Tippenhauer, N.O.: Towards formal security analysis of industrial control systems. In: Proceedings of the 2017 ACM on Asia Conference on Computer and Communications Security, pp. 114–126 (2017)
44. Rose, S.W., Borchert, O., Mitchell, S., Connelly, S.: Zero trust architecture. Technical report, NIST (2020)
45. Saha, A.K., Chowdhury, S., Chowdhury, S.P., Crossley, P.A.: Modeling and performance analysis of a microturbine as a distributed energy resource. IEEE Trans. Energy Convers. **24**(2), 529–538 (2009)
46. Boudghene Stambouli, A., Traversa, E.: Solid oxide fuel cells (SOFCs): a review of an environmentally clean and efficient source of energy. Renew. Sustain. Energy Rev. **6**(5), 433–455 (2002)
47. Tuong, F., Wolff, B.: Deeply integrating C11 code support into Isabelle/PIDE. In: Monahan, R., Prevosto, V., Proença, J. (eds.) F-IDE@FM 2019, Porto, Portugal, 7th October 2019. EPTCS, vol. 310, pp. 13–28 (2019)
48. Vakulchuk, R., Overland, I., Scholten, D.: Renewable energy and geopolitics: a review. Renew. Sustain. Energy Rev. **122**, 109547 (2020)
49. Wendzel, S., Tonejc, J., Kaur, J., Kobekova, A.: Cyber security of smart buildings. In: Security and Privacy in Cyber-Physical Systems: Foundations, Principles and Applications, pp. 327–351 (2017)
50. Wenzel, M.: Structured induction proofs in Isabelle/Isar. In: Borwein, J.M., Farmer, W.M. (eds.) MKM 2006. LNCS (LNAI), vol. 4108, pp. 17–30. Springer, Heidelberg (2006). https://doi.org/10.1007/11812289_3
51. Wenzel, M.: Isabelle/jEdit as IDE for domain-specific formal languages and informal text documents. In: Masci, P., Monahan, R., Prevosto, V. (eds.) Proceedings 4th Workshop on Formal Integrated Development Environment, Oxford, England, 14 July 2018. EPTCS, vol. 284, pp. 71–84 (2018)
52. Wenzel, M.: Interaction with formal mathematical documents in Isabelle/PIDE. In: Kaliszyk, C., Brady, E., Kohlhase, A., Sacerdoti Coen, C. (eds.) CICM 2019. LNCS (LNAI), vol. 11617, pp. 1–15. Springer, Cham (2019). https://doi.org/10.1007/978-3-030-23250-4_1
53. Wikipedia: Aurora Generator Test. https://en.wikipedia.org/wiki/Aurora_Generator_Test
54. Woodcock, J., Hughes, A.: Unifying theories of parallel programming. In: George, C., Miao, H. (eds.) ICFEM 2002. LNCS, vol. 2495, pp. 24–37. Springer, Heidelberg (2002). https://doi.org/10.1007/3-540-36103-0_5
55. Yaacoub, J.-P.A., Salman, O., Noura, H.N., Kaaniche, N., Chehab, A., Malli, M.: Cyber-physical systems security: limitations, issues and future trends. Microprocess. Microsyst. **77**, 103201 (2020)
56. Yadav, G., Paul, K.: Architecture and security of SCADA systems: a review. Int. J. Crit. Infrastruct. Prot. **34**, 100433 (2021)
57. Ye, J., et al.: A review of cyber-physical security for photovoltaic systems. IEEE J. Emerging Sel. Top. Power Electron. **10**(4), 4879–4901 (2021)
58. Ye, K., Foster, S., Woodcock, J.: Automated reasoning for probabilistic sequential programs with theorem proving. In: Fahrenberg, U., Gehrke, M., Santocanale, L., Winter, M. (eds.) RAMiCS 2021. LNCS, vol. 13027, pp. 465–482. Springer, Cham (2021). https://doi.org/10.1007/978-3-030-88701-8_28
59. Zhan, B.: Compositional verification of interacting systems using event monads. In: Andronick, J., de Moura, L. (eds.) 13th International Conference, ITP 2022, 7–10 August 2022, Haifa, Israel. LIPIcs. Schloss Dagstuhl - Leibniz-Zentrum für Informatik (2022)

Provable Determinism for Software in Cyber-Physical Systems

Marcus Rossel[1]([✉]) [iD], Shaokai Jerry Lin[2] [iD], Marten Lohstroh[2] [iD],
Jeronimo Castrillon[1] [iD], and Andrés Goens[3,4] [iD]

[1] TU Dresden, Dresden, Germany
{marcus.rossel,jeronimo.castrillon}@tu-dresden.de
[2] UC Berkeley, Berkeley, USA
{shaokai,marten}@berkeley.edu
[3] The University of Edinburgh, Edinburgh, UK
[4] University of Amsterdam, Amsterdam, Netherlands
a.goens@uva.nl

Abstract. In Cyber-Physical Systems (CPS), concurrently executing software components interact with each other and the physical environment to deliver functionality that is often safety-critical and time-sensitive. Verifying the correctness of the joint behavior of concurrent software components, however, is challenging. It is helpful to eliminate nondeterminism in the software, at the level of the programming model, and provide first-class programming constructs for expressing timed behavior. The Lingua Franca (LF) coordination language achieves this through the use of the Reactor model as its underlying model of computation. In this paper, we present the first formal operational semantics for the Reactor model, and prove its key properties of progress and determinism. The Reactor model and its associated proofs are fully mechanized in the Lean theorem prover. As an operational model, our semantics are close to the intuition for implementation and a helpful reference. The computational objects of the Reactor model are formalized in a modular fashion, which provides insights into the different structural properties of the model, and their effect on execution behavior.

1 Introduction

Cyber-physical systems (CPS) are systems where computational, digital components have integrated physical capabilities and interact with the physical world [4]. Designing and programming these systems brings about multiple challenges. The software has to make decisions about how to affect the physical environment, and the system has to deliver the intended behavior at the correct time. Describing the timed behavior of interacting digital components is one of the main challenges of modeling CPS [2,18,55], and are the subject of study of entire subfields, like timed automata [3] or the more general hybrid automata [22].

© The Author(s), under exclusive license to Springer Nature Switzerland AG 2024
A. Reynolds and S. Tasiran (Eds.): VSTTE 2023, LNCS 14095, pp. 85–107, 2024.
https://doi.org/10.1007/978-3-031-66064-1_6

It is much easier to model CPS and design algorithms for them, if the behavior of the software can be understood as a function of the behavior in the physical environment. But for this to be true, the software has to respond deterministically to inputs from the physical environment. With the software in CPS being increasingly concurrent, due to the use of multi-core, distributed, and networked system architectures, sophisticated coordination is required to ensure determinism in the software. Considering this kind of coordination as part of the application logic can lead to software that is brittle and complex, and tends to make the software less modular and more difficult to understand. Deterministic models of computation, which eliminate nondeterminism by construction, are an effective way to address this problem [19,30,31]. Such models have proven very useful in practice, particularly for the construction of CPS software [21,25,29].

Lingua Franca[1] (LF) [37] is a concrete open-source framework for programming CPS that has recently been gaining traction. The LF runtime enables deterministic concurrency without sacrificing performance [40], and the programming model has an explicit notion of time [32]. At the core of LF is a model of computation, the Reactor model [35,36,38], which offers deterministic timed semantics.

The Reactor model already has well-specified semantics, which ought to serve both as a specification for designing languages and be useful for reasoning about concrete programs. However, they are defined with complicated denotational semantics: using a superdense model of time [39], the semantics are defined through fixpoints of an ultrametric space [14]. In particular, the semantics are neither close to the implementation nor intuitive for programmers to understand. This is mitigated, in part, by the fact that parts of the specification are given as algorithms [35,36]. While the algorithms are useful for implementers, they lack the generality of a fully abstract operational semantics.

In this paper we consider an alternative formalization of the semantics of the Reactor model, using operational semantics [49]. Operational semantics are simpler to understand, while remaining generic – they don't tie the specification to a concrete implementation. For reasons like these, they have become widespread for defining the semantics of programming languages [45,46,57]. We define small-step operational semantics for the Reactor model, providing a foundation to the programming model that is simple and intuitive, yet rigorous.

With these operational semantics, we prove two key properties of the model: *progress* (execution does not get "stuck") and *determinism*. The model and its associated proofs are fully mechanized[2] in the Lean theorem prover [41]. This mechanization provides several advantages. First, it forces us to be precise about otherwise implicit definitions and assumptions, which is especially important in the context of verifying computation [28]. In particular, we find multiple ways in which the denotational semantics in [35,36] are imprecise, and make them precise. Second, it serves as a thorough documentation of the semantics, which provides insights into different structural properties of the model, and

---

[1] https://www.lf-lang.org/.

[2] https://github.com/lf-lang/reactor-model.

their consequences on execution behavior. For example, we require reactors to be finite to prove progress, while the proof of determinism does not need this restriction. Finally, it aids the process of working on modifications and extensions of the model, by uncovering where existing proofs break.

The rest of this paper is structured as follows. Section 2 introduces the Reactor model by example and formalizes its computational objects. The operational semantics governing the execution model are given in Sect. 3, and its key properties are proven in Sect. 4. Finally, Sect. 5 covers related work and Sect. 6 concludes the paper.

2 Reactors

The Reactor model is a concurrent model of computation. Computation is encapsulated in *reactors*, the most fundamental structure of the model. To introduce reactors and their components informally, we walk through a model inspired by the Ingenuity Mars Helicopter[3] as shown in Fig. 1. The helicopter uses multiple sensors, including different cameras which produce images that have to be processed. A controller then decides how to navigate based on these inputs and its internal logic, and controls actuators, like motors, to do so.

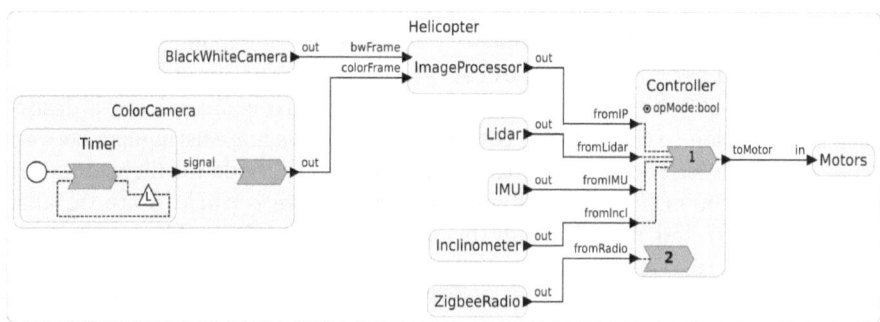

Fig. 1. Reactor-based model of the Ingenuity Mars Helicopter.

Each rounded rectangle in Fig. 1 represents a reactor. We have expanded certain reactors like **ColorCamera** to show their components, while collapsing others like **ImageProcessor** where the details aren't relevant. The **ColorCamera** reactor models a camera which is continuously polled for new frames which are then communicated to the **ImageProcessor** . This communication is achieved by *connections* (depicted as bold lines) of *ports* (depicted as filled triangles). Concretely, the **ColorCamera** communicates frames via its **out** port, which has a connection to the **ImageProcessor** 's **colorFrame** port. Thus, when a value is set on **out** it is propagated to **colorFrame** . Ports are read from and written to

---

[3] See https://www.youtube.com/watch?v=D-Y6H0GMtbM&t=465s.

by *reactions* (depicted as chevrons). Reactions are routines which can read and write values from and to different components called their *sources* and *effects*, which they must declare explicitly (depicted as dashed lines). When a source that is marked as a *trigger* has an available value, the reaction is *triggered*, executing the procedure which may read the values of its sources and set the values of its effects. In the example, the reaction contained in `ColorCamera` would be the routine responsible for actually reading the frame from the camera. It declares the `out` port as an effect, as it wants to write the frame to that port. It also declares the `signal` port of the *nested* `Timer` reactor as a source. That is, reactors can be nested in other reactors and thus form a tree structure. In fact, the entire model is represented by the single `Helicopter` reactor which contains all other reactors. The `Timer` reactor is used to implement polling by setting a value on its `signal` port every 33 milliseconds, which in turn triggers the `ColorCamera`'s reaction. To create an event delayed by 33 milliseconds, a *logical action* is used (depicted as a triangle containing the letter L). Whenever the `Timer`'s reaction executes, it *schedules* an event for the logical action with the given delay. After the specified amount of time, the logical action makes its value available which in turn triggers the reaction again. The circle shape contained in the `Timer` depicts a special kind of trigger that is present only at startup to bootstrap the process. Thus, upon starting the helicopter, the `Timer`'s output port periodically triggers the `ColorCamera`'s reaction which then supplies a steady stream of frames via its output port. These frames are propagated to and processed by the `ImageProcessor`, which finally communicates its results to the `Controller`. The `Controller` processes various inputs including the output of a `ZigbeeRadio`. This radio can be used to communicate a desired mode of operation to the `Controller`. For example, we may distinguish between a manual mode for testing on earth and an automatic mode for flight on Mars. The selected mode is stored locally in the `opMode` *state variable*. State variables can be accessed and modified only by a reactor's reactions. Thus, one of the `Controller`'s reactions is used to set the `opMode` based on the `ZigbeeRadio`'s input, while the other reads the `opMode` to determine which sensor values to include in its navigation algorithm.

The rest of this section will introduce reactors formally. As our formalization is mechanized in Lean, we express the following definitions in the language of Lean's underlying type theory [13,41], which is derived from the Calculus of Inductive Constructions (CIC) [16,17,42]. For simplicity of the presentation, we omit certain details and generally use more traditional mathematical (set-theoretic) syntax. However, the full details can be found in the accompanying mechanization, with the appendix linking to all presented definitions.

2.1   Basic Reactors

Formally, we define reactors in terms of axioms, similar to how algebraic structures like groups are defined in conventional mathematics. The canonical way to define objects in terms of axioms in Lean is by using type classes [54].[4] Thus, we define a hierarchy of type classes for reactors which successively add axioms until we arrive at what we call *proper* reactors. We split the axioms of reactors into multiple type classes, as different parts of the formalization require varying degrees of constraints.

At the base of this type class hierarchy is the class of (basic) Reactors. It states that a reactor contains the following identifiable components: input ports, output ports, state variables, actions, reactions and nested reactors. By "identifiable" we mean that every component in a reactor has an associated identifier of some opaque ID type, which can be used to reference and obtain a component from a reactor. Formally:

Definition 1 (Reactor). A type α is a Reactor type if it has a partial function get?, which to any given element of α, component kind cpt and identifier associates an object of type cptType(cpt, α). In Lean:

```
class Reactor (α : Type) where
    get? : α → (cpt : Component) → ID → Option (cptType cpt α)
```

Lean uses ML-syntax and currying, which means that "cptType cpt α" is the function application cptType(cpt, α). The type Option(A) extends a type A by the distinguished element none. Thus, we consider get? to be a partial function (a function only defined on a subset of its inputs) by returning none when the function is undefined for a given input. The Component type defines labels for the kinds of components listed above with the cptType function associating a type with each of these labels:

$$\text{Component} = \{\text{inp}, \text{out}, \text{stv}, \text{act}, \text{rcn}, \text{rtr}\}$$

$$\text{cptType}(cpt, \alpha) := \begin{cases} \alpha & \text{if } cpt = \text{rtr} \\ \text{Reaction} & \text{if } cpt = \text{rcn} \\ \text{Value} & \text{otherwise} \end{cases}$$

Thus, for example, get?(r, rcn, i) $= n$ means that reactor r contains a reaction n identified by identifier i. It is important to note that the notion of containment of a component in a reactor induced by get? is considered to be "flat". That is, components contained in nested reactors are not considered to be contained in the parent reactor. For example, Fig. 2 shows that the reaction contained in the Timer reactor from Fig. 1 is not considered to be contained in the ColorCamera reactor.[5]

Reactions. The component kinds inp, out, stv and act are similar by their associated type being Value. Thus, we collectively call them ValuedComponents.

---

[4] Type classes are similar to (but more powerful than) interfaces in Java, traits in Rust, protocols in Swift, etc.

[5] It *would* hold if ColorCamera also directly contained the reaction n and identified it by i. In Sect. 2.2 we eliminate such duplicate identification with *hierarchical* reactors.

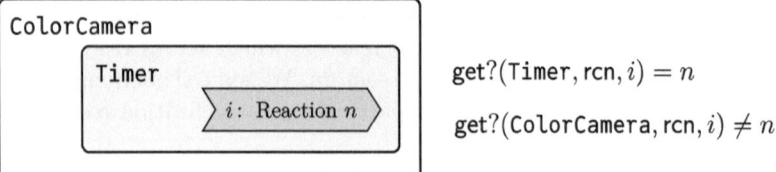

Fig. 2. Example of "flatness" of get?.

The Value type is an opaque type (in the same way as ID) of values with a distinguished absent element. Reactions, on the other hand, as the smallest units of computation in the Reactor model, are essentially functions with additional structure.

Definition 2 (Reaction). A *reaction* is a structure (tuple) of the form:[6]
```
structure Reaction where
    sources  : Set (ValuedComponent × ID)
    effects  : Set (ValuedComponent × ID)
    triggers : Set (ValuedComponent × ID)
    priority : Priority
    body     : (ValuedComponent → ID → Option Value) → List Change
```

We use the names of structures' fields to refer to the respective values. For example, given a reaction n we write sources(n) to denote the reaction's sources. The set of sources identifies components which are inputs to the reaction, and the set of effects are its outputs. A subset of the sources, called triggers, is used in the execution model to determine whether a reaction should be executed, with the priority affecting the order in which different reactions are executed.[7] At the heart of a reaction is its body, which is the function defining its behavior. Its input is a map providing the values of its sources. As an output, it returns *changes*, which formalize how a reaction affects its effects:

Definition 3 (Change). A Change combines an identified component with the value that should be assigned to it. Formally:[8]
```
structure Change where
    cpt : ValuedComponent
    id  : ID
    val : Value
```

This can be seen as a special case of algebraic effects [26,48], as will become clearer in Sect. 3 when we define the execution semantics. We note that our rigorous definition of reaction bodies fills a gap in the formal treatment of reactions in [35,36], where they are defined simply as "executable code".

---

[6] This definition omits certain edge cases for the sake of simplicity. For example, state variables are allowed as a sources, but not as a triggers.

[7] The Priority type is an opaque type with a partial order.

[8] This definition is slightly simplified. The type of the value actually depends on the specific valued component. For act the associated value has type Time × Value.

Connections. Connections propagate values between reactors' ports. Notably, connections can only be established between nested reactors which live in the same parent reactor. We don't formalize connections directly, but instead take the same approach as [35] and replace them with the notion of a *relay reaction* as demonstrated in Fig. 3. A relay reaction is a reaction whose sole purpose is to propagate a value from one port to another.

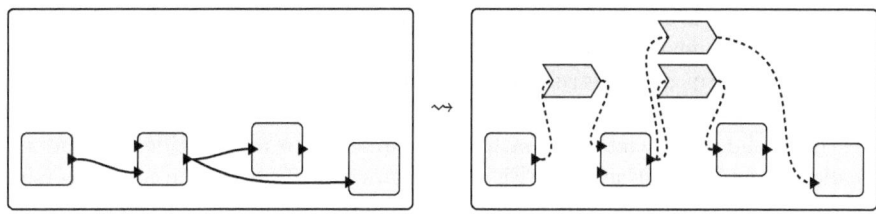

Fig. 3. Example of replacing connections by relay reactions.

Definition 4 (Relay Reaction). Let r be a reactor with nested reactors r_1 and r_2 and c be a connection from output port o of r_1 to input port i of r_2. A reaction n is a *relay reaction* for c, if:

- n is directly contained in r.
- $\mathsf{sources}(n) = \mathsf{triggers}(n) = \{(\mathsf{out}, o)\}$ and $\mathsf{effects}(n) = \{(\mathsf{inp}, i)\}$.
- $\mathsf{body}(n)$ writes the value of (out, o) to (inp, i).
- $\mathsf{priority}(n)$ is incomparable to the priorities of all other reactions in r.

The last requirement is crucial. As a connection propagates its values *immediately*, a corresponding relay reaction must be able to propagate its value at any time, as well. As a result, it must have a priority which allows it to execute independently of any other reaction in the same reactor.[9] In [35] this is achieved by defining a special priority which is only available to reactions for which it is known that they do not touch the reactor's state. This restriction is required as they define reactions in such a way that all state variables of their parent reactor are implicitly part of their sources and effects, and therefore all (normal) reactions in a reactor need to be totally ordered by their priority to retain determinism. In our formalization, this edge case is avoided by making state variables *explicit* dependencies of reactions and defining rules for the ordering of reactions' priorities (Definition 8). Thus, relay reactions can be defined without requiring special considerations.

---

[9] This also implies that connections are only truly reducible to relay reactions if the Priority type has an incomparable element.

2.2   Hierarchical Reactors

Recall that nested reactors allow us to declare an entire system of reactors hierarchically, as a single root reactor that contains a tree of nested reactors. To reason formally about nested reactors and the resulting hierarchical structure, basic reactors are insufficient, as their get? function does not impose any structure on the components of reactors. For example, in basic reactors multiple components can share the same identifier, and the graph of reactors induced by nesting can form any directed graph.[10] As we intend to use identifiers to uniquely refer to components, we next constrain identifiers to be unique – this also forces the reactor graph to form a tree structure. We achieve this by forcing all components contained (arbitrarily deeply nested) in a reactor to be accessible by a unique path from the root reactor. A path from a reactor to an identified component is called a *membership witness*. Figure 4 shows how each step in a membership witness is a proof that we can get from one reactor to the next by direct nesting, ending in a proof that the desired identified component is contained in the final reactor.

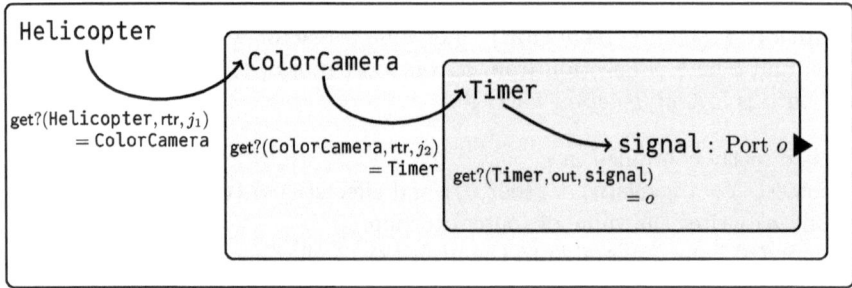

Fig. 4. Membership witness of the output port identified as signal for the Helicopter root reactor.

Definition 5 (Member). Formally, we define membership witnesses over a reactor type α inductively [17] as follows:

```
inductive Member (cpt : Component) (i : ID) : α → Type
   | final  : get? r cpt i = some o → Member cpt i r
   | nested : get? r₁ .rtr j = some r₂ → Member cpt i r₂ →
              Member cpt i r₁
```

In this Lean snippet, we assume that α is a basic reactor type, and we define a Member inductively as a function of a component kind *cpt*, an identifier i and a reactor of type α. This inductive definition has two cases. The **final** (base) case has as condition that get?(r, cpt, i) is defined. The **nested** (inductive) case requires that the (root) reactor r_1 directly contains a nested reactor r_2 for

---

[10] For example, we can construct a self loop by letting get?$(r, \mathrm{rtr}, i) = r$.

which we already have a membership witness of i of kind cpt. To construct a membership witness, we provide proofs of these conditions as arguments to the constructors, which are just functions by the principle of Propositions as Types [45,56]. By the same principle, a membership witness of i of kind cpt in r is then a term of type $\mathsf{Member}(cpt, i, r)$.[11]

Definition 6 (Hierarchical Reactors). A Hierarchical reactor type is then a (basic) Reactor type where there exists at most one membership witness for any given identified component:

```
class Hierarchical (α) extends Reactor α where
    unique_ids : ∀ r cpt i (m₁ m₂ : Member cpt i r), m₁ = m₂
```

While hierarchical reactors impose structure on reactors, we yet need to define tools to aid formal reasoning over them. When defining properties over reactors, it is common to refer to components which are located *somewhere* in the tree of a given root reactor, but not necessarily in the same parent reactor. For example in Sect. 2.3 we define that "no two distinct reactions share an input port as effect." This requires us to be able to refer to any two reactions in the reactor tree. The get? function is ill-suited for this purpose, as its notion of containment is flat. That is, it only considers components *directly* nested in the reactor on which it is called.

Hierarchical reactors give us a natural way of extending the get? function such that we can refer to components anywhere in a reactor tree. For this, we first define the object of a membership witness to be the value of its identified component. For example if we have a membership witness $m : \mathsf{Member}(\mathsf{inp}, i, r)$ and the input port identified by i has the value 5, then we define $\mathsf{object}(m) = 5$. We then define the partial function obj? which extends get? to work on an entire reactor tree:

Definition 7 (Extended Accessor).

$$\mathsf{obj?} : \alpha \rightarrow (cpt : \mathsf{Component}) \rightarrow \mathsf{ID} \rightarrow \mathsf{Option}(\mathsf{cptType}(cpt, \alpha))$$

$$\mathsf{obj?}(r, cpt, i) := \begin{cases} \mathsf{object}(m) & \text{if } m : \mathsf{Member}(cpt, i, r) \text{ exists} \\ \mathsf{none} & \text{if no membership witness exists} \end{cases}$$

Thus, for example, $\mathsf{obj?}(r, \mathsf{inp}, i) = 5$ means that somewhere in the tree of root reactor r there exists an input port identified by i with value 5. Note that this function is not computable in general, as we cannot decide the existence of a membership witness for an arbitrary hierarchical reactor type. For reactors containing only finitely many components it is easily computable, though.[12]

Hierarchical reactors are already vastly more useful than basic reactors in that they allow us to *define* many useful properties of reactors – often by using

---

[11] We note that Member lives in Type, not in Prop as we need to be able to distinguish different paths to the same identified component. If Member were a Prop, those paths would all be considered equal by proof irrelevance.

[12] For example, by a simple tree traversal on the finite reactor tree.

the extended accessor. For example, the entire execution model is defined over hierarchical reactors. To actually *prove* properties like progress and determinism, we need to add additional constraints provided in the following section. It is worth noting that formal treatment of identifier uniqueness, accessor functions and the distinction between properties needed for definitions as opposed to proofs are glossed over in the previous formal literature about the Reactor model [35, 36].

2.3   Proper Reactors

The class of *proper* reactors adds all axioms which are necessary to ensure that reactor execution can be defined in a way that results in deterministic behavior.

Definition 8 (Proper Reactors). A Proper reactor type is a hierarchical reactor type with the following additional properties:[13]

(1) Unique Inputs. No two distinct reactions share an input port as effect.

(2) Ordered Priorities. The priorities of any two distinct reactions in the same reactor are totally ordered if one of the following holds:

– The reactions share an effect.
– The reactions share a state variable as dependency which is an effect for at least one of them.

(3) Valid Dependencies. Reactions only declare *valid* sources and effects. For a reaction n contained directly in a reactor r, validity is defined as follows:

– Input ports of r are valid sources for n.
– Output ports of r are valid effects for n.
– State variables of r are valid sources and effects for n.
– Actions and state variables of r are valid sources and effects for n.
– Input ports of reactors directly nested in r are valid effects for n.
– Output ports of reactors directly nested in r are valid sources for n.

Notably, the ordering of priorities is not explicitly considered in [35,36] and the restrictions on state variables are new, as we now treat them as explicit dependencies.

2.4   The Complete Type Class Hierarchy

The previous section omits some details of proper reactors. Namely, the class of proper reactors extends hierarchical reactors, as well as three others. These additional classes impose constraints which are not necessarily characteristic of reactors but are used for proving progress and determinism. In Fig. 5 we show the full hierarchy of classes followed by brief explanations of each class.

---

[13] This is a simplification. See Sect. 2.4 for the full picture.

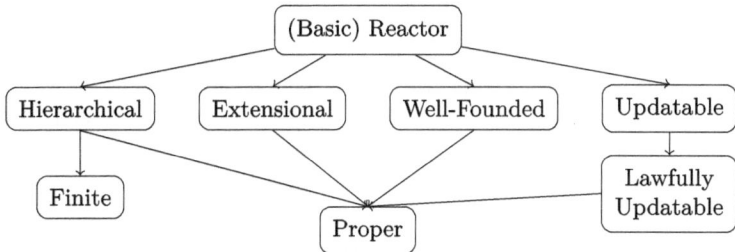

Fig. 5. Complete hierarchy of type classes used to formalize reactors.

Extensional Reactors. A reactor type is called *extensional* if its reactors are completely characterized by their components:

$$\forall r_1, r_2 : (r_1 = r_2) \leftrightarrow (\forall \, cpt, i : \mathsf{get?}(r_1, cpt, i) = \mathsf{get?}(r_2, cpt, i))$$

Well-Founded Reactors. A reactor type is called *well-founded* if the direct nesting relation $\exists i : \mathsf{get?}(r_2, \mathsf{rtr}, i) = r_1$ over r_1 and r_2 is well-founded [23,43]. That is, there are no infinitely deeply nested reactors.[14] This allows us to perform well-founded induction on reactors.

(Lawfully) Updatable Reactors. A reactor type α is called *updatable* if it has a function $\mathsf{update} : \alpha \rightarrow \mathsf{ValuedComponent} \rightarrow \mathsf{ID} \rightarrow \mathsf{Value} \rightarrow \alpha$. It is called *lawfully updatable* if this function satisfies the intuitive notion of setting a given identified component to a given value.

Finite Reactors. A hierarchical reactor type is called *finite* if each reac tor contains only finitely many components. That is, the set $\{\, i \mid \exists o : \mathsf{obj?}(r, cpt, i) = o \,\}$ is finite for all r and cpt.

   We have thus defined reactors in a modular way, with the different properties shown in Fig. 5. Overall, defining reactors this way serves two purposes. First, it formalizes implicit assumptions, like the uniqueness of identifiers or the proper ordering of reaction priorities. And second, it factors properties of reactors in a way that allows us to distinguish the necessary assumptions for main properties, like progress and determinism, as we will see in Sect. 4.

3   Operational Semantics

Having defined reactors, we define their execution in this section by using operational semantics. We first consider the notions of time and dependencies, which are central to the Reactor model. We distinguish between *physical* (wall-clock)

---

[14] A well-founded reactor can still contain infinitely many nested reactors by having an infinite branching factor.

time and *logical time* [21,27,33]. Logical time is measured in terms of superdense-time *tags*, which consist of a *time value* and a *microstep* [5,34,39]. Execution of reactions (including writing to ports) and propagation of values via connections are considered "logically instantaneous", that is, they don't advance logical time. Thus, it is possible and typical for multiple reactions to execute at the same logical time. In this case, it is critical to determine an order for executing these reactions, which ensures that each reaction's dependencies have already finished executing before it itself executes. For this purpose, we define a *dependency relation* between reactions, based on their sources, effects and priorities:

Definition 9 (Dependency Relation). A reaction n_1 *is a dependency of* a reaction n_2 in reactor r, written $n_1 <_r n_2$, if one of the following holds:

1. n_1 and n_2 live in the same reactor and $\mathsf{priority}(n_1) > \mathsf{priority}(n_2)$.
2. There exist i and a $cpt \neq \mathsf{stv}$, such that $(cpt, i) \in \mathsf{effects}(n_1) \cap \mathsf{sources}(n_2)$.[15]
3. There exists a reaction n with $n_1 <_r n$ and $n <_r n_2$. That is, $<_r$ is transitive.

While reactions execute at a single instant in logical time, for the model to be useful, they also need to be able to communicate *across* logical time. Thus, we introduce *logical actions*, which allow reactions to schedule communication of values at specific logical time points in the future. Actions are similar to ports in that they carry values and can be read and written to by reactions, but differ from them in that they hold a given value at a specified future logical time. Thus, logical actions are the means by which future events are scheduled from *within* a reactor. Events can also be created asynchronously by the environment through *physical actions*. Such actions are not scheduled by reactions, but instead initiated by external components like sensors. Aside from how their events are created, physical actions and logical actions are handled equally in the model. The tags of events that originate from physical actions are *inputs* to the system. Hence, we do not need to model them as part of the semantics to conclude that the behavior triggered by such inputs is deterministic. For the sake of simplicity, we therefore do not include physical actions in our semantics.

Having understood the notions of time and dependencies, we can define execution as a relation that determines how to construct valid sequences of *execution states*. An execution state is a structure which adds context to a reactor for the purpose of managing its execution. More precisely:

Definition 10 (Execution State). An *execution state* over a hierarchical reactor type α is a structure of the following form:

```
structure State (α) where
    rtr      : α
    tag      : Tag
    progress : Set ID
    events   : ID → Tag → Option Value
```

---

[15] When i is a state variable we get a dependency by combining Property 2 of proper reactors with Case 1 of $<_r$.

The rtr is the root reactor of the reactor system we want to execute. The tag holds the current logical time tag of the execution, where Tag is the type of logical time tags. The progress set indicates which reactions have already been processed at the current tag, while the events map keeps track of which action has which value at any given tag.

Definition 11 (Execution Relation). The operational semantics of reactor execution are then given by the *execution relation* $\downarrow^*$ over execution states. It is the reflexive, transitive closure of the execution step relation $\downarrow$ as shown in Fig. 6.

$$\frac{}{s \downarrow^* s} \qquad \frac{s_1 \downarrow s_2 \quad s_2 \downarrow^* s_3}{s_1 \downarrow^* s_3} \qquad \frac{\text{Allows}(s, n) \quad \neg\text{Triggers}(s, n)}{s \downarrow \text{record}(s, n)} \;\; \text{skip-step}$$

$$\frac{\text{Allows}(s, n) \quad \text{Triggers}(s, n) \quad s -[\text{output}(s, n)] \rightarrow s'}{s \downarrow \text{record}(s', n)} \;\; \text{exec-step}$$

$$\frac{\text{Closed}(s) \quad \text{NextTag}(s, g) \quad \text{Refresh}(\text{rtr}(s), r, \text{actions}(s, g))}{s \downarrow \langle r, g, \emptyset, \text{events}(s) \rangle} \;\; \text{time-step}$$

Fig. 6. Operational semantics of reactor execution.

The *skip-step* and *exec-step* rules formalize how to process a single reaction. As they occur logically instantaneously, we collectively call them "instantaneous steps". In both cases, the reaction needs to be "allowed" to be processed, which is the case if all of n's dependencies have been processed, but n itself has not yet been processed. More formally:

Definition 12 (Allows Relation). An execution state s *allows* a reaction n to be processed, written $\text{Allows}(s, n)$, if $\{ n' \mid n' <_{\text{rtr}(s)} n \} \subseteq \text{progress}(s)$ and $n \notin \text{progress}(s)$.

The choice of instantaneous step then depends on whether the reaction is currently triggered.

Definition 13 (Triggering Relation). A reaction n is triggered at a given execution state s, written $\text{Triggers}(s, n)$, if at least one of n's triggers is present. That is, $\exists (cpt, i) \in \text{triggers}(n) : \text{obj?}(\text{rtr}(s), cpt, i) \neq \text{absent}$.

If a reaction n is not triggered, *skip-step* applies, which records n as being processed without executing it. That is, the execution state remains unchanged except for its progress which becomes $\text{progress}(s) \cup \{n\}$. If on the other hand n is triggered, *exec-step* applies, which executes the reaction and applies its resulting changes to the current execution state. The latter is formalized by the "update relation" $s -[...] \rightarrow s'$, which is satisfied if s and s' are equal up to applying a given list of changes. For the sake of brevity, we omit the details of this relation, but note that its definition is complicated by the Frame Problem [11]. That is, most of the difficulty in defining this relation arises from having to define what does *not* change when applying a change.

The given definitions of *skip-step* and *exec-step* give rise to nondeterministic choice in the semantics: at a given execution state, there may be multiple reactions which satisfy the conditions of either of these rules. The choice of which reaction to process next is then nondeterministic, which models the concurrency in the system. The fact that this degree of nondeterminism does not affect the resulting execution state at each time step is a key result of our semantics (see Sect. 4.2). Once all reactions have been processed at the current time tag, we call an execution state *closed*. A *time-step* can then occur, if there exists some future tag at which an event is scheduled:

Definition 14 (Next-Tag Relation). A tag g is the *next tag* of an execution state s, written $\mathsf{NextTag}(s, g)$, if it is the smallest tag satisfying $\mathsf{tag}(s) < g$ and $\exists\, i : \mathsf{events}(s)(i, g) \neq \mathsf{none}$.

Performing a *time-step* on s consists of advancing $\mathsf{tag}(s)$ to the next tag, setting $\mathsf{progress}(s) := \emptyset$, clearing the values of all ports and setting the values of all actions to the values given by $\mathsf{events}(s)$ for the new tag. The last two steps are handled by the $\mathsf{Refresh}$ relation.

Definition 15 (Refresh Relation). A hierarchical reactor r_1 *refreshes to* r_2 with action values $v : \mathsf{ID} \to \mathsf{Option}(\mathsf{Value})$, written $\mathsf{Refresh}(r_1, r_2, v)$, if:

- Inputs are cleared: $\forall\, i : \mathsf{obj}?(r_1, \mathsf{inp}, i) \neq \mathsf{none} \to \mathsf{obj}?(r_2, \mathsf{inp}, i) = \mathsf{absent}$
- Outputs are cleared: $\forall\, i : \mathsf{obj}?(r_1, \mathsf{out}, i) \neq \mathsf{none} \to \mathsf{obj}?(r_2, \mathsf{out}, i) = \mathsf{absent}$
- Action values are set: $\mathsf{obj}?(r_2, \mathsf{act}) = v$
- State variables are preserved: $\mathsf{obj}?(r_2, \mathsf{stv}) = \mathsf{obj}?(r_1, \mathsf{stv})$
- r_1 and r_2 are *structurally equivalent*. Intuitively, this means they contain the same components arranged equally and differ only by their values. The precise definition is rather technical and is therefore omitted here.[16]

4 Progress and Determinism

One of the major claims of the Reactor model is that, despite a certain degree of nondeterministic choice, its execution model is deterministic. In this section, we substantiate this claim and prove the following theorems over proper reactors:

Progress. There exists an execution step from any non-terminal execution state if and only if its reactor's dependency graph is acyclic.

---

[16] Cf. `Reactor.Equivalent` in the mechanization.

Determinism. All executions of a proper reactor up to the same point result in the same state. That is, the nondeterministic order of execution steps does not affect an execution's outcome.

We provide proof sketches for these theorems here; the full proofs can be found in our mechanization. The appendix lists the names of theorems and lemmas as they can be found in the mechanization.

4.1   Progress

In the literature surrounding the Reactor model, the definition of reactors usually includes the assumption that their dependency graphs are acyclic [35, 36].[17] Yet, our formalization does not require this. In this section, we show that an acyclic dependency graph is only necessary to ensure that execution of a reactor can make progress. In fact, acyclicity of the dependency graph *characterizes* the ability to make progress. To prove this theorem, we first formalize its statement.

Definition 16 (Progress Property).   We say that a reactor r can make progress, that is, has the *progress property*, if for all non-terminal execution states s starting at r there exists a state s' such that $s \downarrow s'$.

Definition 17 (Terminal State).   An execution state s is *terminal* if progress(s) contains all reactions of rtr(s) and there are no events scheduled after tag(s).

Definition 18 (Dependency Graph).   The *dependency graph* of a reactor r is the directed graph of reactions of r, where there is an edge between reactions n_1 and n_2 if and only if $n_1 <_r n_2$. As the dependency relation is transitive, the dependency graph of r is acyclic if and only if the relation $<_r$ is irreflexive.

Theorem 1 (Progress Theorem).   For all finite proper reactors r, r has the progress property if and only if it has an acyclic dependency graph.

Proof Sketch. We prove both directions independently.

To prove the forward direction we need to show that for any reaction n, n does not depend on itself ($n \not<_r n$). We achieve this by constructing a special non-terminal state s over r whose progress contains all reactions except n. Assuming the progress property for r, we obtain that there exists an execution step starting from s, which by construction of s must be a *skip-step* or *exec-step* of n. In either case, Allows(s, n) must hold, from which one can easily prove that n does not depend on itself.[18]

The backward direction is shown by explicitly constructing an execution step for a given non-terminal state s over reactor r. If s has no unprocessed reactions for the current tag, we can easily construct a *time-step*. Otherwise, we can show by induction on the set of unprocessed reactions that there must exist a reaction

---

[17] This is typically called an "absence of algebraic loops".
[18] The proof of this direction works generally for hierarchical reactors.

which is itself unprocessed, yet has only dependencies which are processed. This proof step works only because r's dependency graph is acyclic. Depending on whether the obtained reaction is triggered or not, we can construct either a *skip-step* or *exec-step* for it.

4.2   Determinism

To formally state the theorem of determinism, we need to formalize the notion of "executions up to the same point". If we have executions $s \downarrow^* s_1$ and $s \downarrow^* s_2$, it is not sufficient to have only $\mathsf{tag}(s_1) = \mathsf{tag}(s_2)$. We also need to ensure that s_1 and s_2 have executed the same reactions within their current tag, that is, have the same $\mathsf{progress}$:

Theorem 2 (Determinism). For all execution states s, s_1, s_2 over proper reactors, we have:

$$s \downarrow^* s_1 \rightarrow s \downarrow^* s_2 \rightarrow \mathsf{tag}(s_1) = \mathsf{tag}(s_2) \rightarrow \mathsf{progress}(s_1) = \mathsf{progress}(s_2) \rightarrow s_1 = s_2$$

Proof Sketch. The proof of this theorem can be divided into two main parts. First, we show that sequences of execution steps must always be structured as alternations of two kinds of subsequences as shown in Fig. 7: (1) a sequence of instantaneous steps covering all reactions and (2) a single time step.

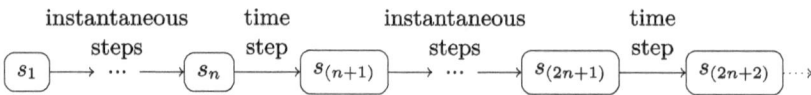

Fig. 7. Structure of executions as alternations of instantaneous steps and time steps.

This can be proven solely based on the structure of the execution rules and does not require the specific properties of proper reactors. Time steps can rather easily be proven deterministic, so what remains to be shown is that subsequences of instantaneous steps (denoted $\downarrow_{i+}$) are deterministic:

Lemma 1 (Instantaneous Determinism). For all execution states s, s_1, s_2 over proper reactors, we have:

$$s \downarrow_{i+} s_1 \rightarrow s \downarrow_{i+} s_2 \rightarrow \mathsf{progress}(s_1) = \mathsf{progress}(s_2) \rightarrow s_1 = s_2$$

This lemma lies at the heart of the proof of determinism. It is shown by induction using the following lemma, which establishes that if a reaction does not depend on another reaction, executing it first preserves the result of execution:

Lemma 2 (Independent Reaction Swap). For all instantaneous execution steps $e_1 : s_1 \downarrow_i s_2$ and $e_2 : s_2 \downarrow_i s_3$ with $\mathsf{rcn}(e_1) \not\prec_{\mathsf{rtr}(s_1)} \mathsf{rcn}(e_2)$, we can construct an execution state s_2' and instantaneous execution steps $e_1' : s_1 \downarrow_i s_2'$ and $e_2' : s_2' \downarrow_i s_3$ such that $\mathsf{rcn}(e_1') = \mathsf{rcn}(e_2)$ and $\mathsf{rcn}(e_2') = \mathsf{rcn}(e_1)$.

We write $\mathsf{rcn}(e)$ to denote the reaction processed by instantaneous execution step e. As the statement of the lemma shows, we explicitly *construct* the swapped execution steps. As part of this construction we need to explicitly construct the new intermediate reactor $\mathsf{rtr}(s_2')$, which is why we need proper reactors to be lawfully updatable. Furthermore, the proof of this lemma builds on many small technical lemmas about independent reactions, which is where the properties of proper reactors are required. For example, they allow us to establish that independent reactions can never write to the same component.

Corollary 1. An immediate consequence of the theorem of determinism is that executions "synchronize" at every time step. That is, if we compare multiple executions we get a diamond structure as shown in Fig. 8. It is an open problem to define execution in such a way that reordering of execution steps can transcend time barriers while retaining determinism.

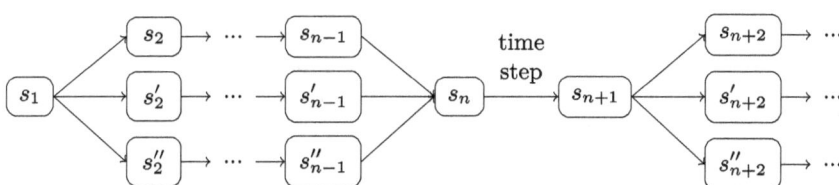

Fig. 8. Synchronization behavior of executions as a result of determinism.

5   Related Work

Concurrency is a central concept in computing in general, and consequently, there are many other well-studied models for describing and understanding concurrency. Petri nets are a staple formal model used for concurrency [44]. They are one of the most general models, specifying little in the way of structure.

On the algebraic side, a family of models called Process Algebras [9] gives algebraic (equational) semantics to concurrent systems. These are particularly useful to build up the semantics compositionally, for example by introducing parallel or synchronous composition operators and specifying how the compound system behaves. Other models have also been put forward, like those based on game semantics [1] which all strive to the a high level of generality, allowing many behaviors that are undesirable in CPS and impossible in reactors. Kahn semantics [25], on the other hand, provide a topological view of deterministic concurrency based on Scott-continuous functions [53]. These models all enable modeling of concurrency, but not necessarily reasoning about time semantics.

Reactors mix concepts from several of these existing models, including actors [15], synchronous languages [50], dataflow [24], and discrete event systems [52]. They do so to enable deterministic, concurrent semantics with an explicit notion of time. Indeed, the Reactor model can also be characterized as a Sparse Synchronous Model [20] and a generalization of the Logical Execution Time (LET) paradigm [33], which has gained a lot of traction in industry.

Of particular interest here are synchronous languages, which are commonly used to program CPS. This includes Signal [7], Lustre [47] and commercial variants like SCADE or (a subset of) Simulink. These languages implement the synchronous/reactive model of computation, which can be seen as a subset of the discrete event semantics that are the basis of the Reactor model [51]. In general, synchronous languages like Lustre or Signal are more fine-grained than the Reactor model and have more restrictive semantics for the computational nodes. They also have a simpler model of time: discrete time, with an assumption of uniformity, as opposed to the superdense time model with an explicit distinction of logical and physical time in the Reactor model. Lustre, for example, forbids the use of unbounded loops and recursive functions. This is done to ensure a realistic synchrony with short response times. Signal similarly assumes an instantaneous execution of the digital logic in the system as well as the communication with the environment. This is in contrast to LF and the Reactor model, which models the execution times of reactions explicitly and allows arbitrary computation through potentially dynamic execution times.

The synchronous languages Lustre [8], Signal [7] and Esterel [10] were all defined with a specified semantics. Lustre's denotational semantics are in the Kahn style [25], which is the same style as the original reactor semantics [36], combined with an ultrametric space to model superdense time [14]. The denotational semantics of Signal are also based on Kahn Networks, but with extensions for their relational nature [6]. Interestingly, as in this paper, *both* Lustre *and* Signal also define operational semantics to be closer to the compiler implementation [7,47], even after having had denotational semantics before. Esterel was first given operational semantics in this style [10].

The operational semantics of Lustre are also mechanized in Coq for the Velus compiler [12]. A key difference is that these semantics (coinductively) reason about entire streams of execution at once, whereas our semantics reason about individual events in a stream. Moreover, Lustre and Signal are concrete languages, whereas the Reactor model is a more abstract model of computation; we formalize neither the concrete LF syntax nor its compiler.

6   Conclusion

LF and its underlying Reactor model enable constructing concurrent yet deterministic software for CPS. They provide primitives for concurrent processes, while enforcing structure through explicit dependencies and time semantics. We provide a rigorous formalization of the semantics in Lean and use it to deliver mechanized proofs of determinism and progress. Our proof of determinism shows that the parallelism exposed by LF is safe, and our proof of progress provides a clear explanation as to why LF can only accept programs without causality loops. The operational semantics that we provide is simple and intuitive.

We envision that our work may prove useful for the construction of verified compilers and runtime implementations. This could enable verification of CPS software with a small trusted computing base (TCB) through Lean. Our formalization could also serve as tool for prototyping possible extensions of the core Reactor model and evaluating their consequences. An example of this would be developing a model of *mutations*, which are reactions that can change the structure of a reactor. The current mechanization already includes mutations as components, but ignores them in the execution model, as they require a significant reconsideration of the proof of determinism.

Acknowledgments. We thank the anonymous reviewers for their feedback which greatly improved the clarity of the manuscript. This work was funded in part by the Engineering and Physical Sciences Research Council (EPSRC), through grant reference EP/V038699/1, as well as the German Federal Ministry of Education and Research (BMBF) as part of the Software Campus (01IS12051) and the program "Souverän. Digital. Vernetzt.", joint project 6G-life (16KISK001K). This work was also supported in part by the National Science Foundation (NSF), awards #CNS-1836601 (Reconciling Safety with the Internet) and #CNS-2233769 (Consistency vs. Availability in Cyber-Physical Systems) and the iCyPhy Research Center (Industrial Cyber-Physical Systems), supported by Denso, Siemens, and Toyota.

A   Definitions and Theorems in the Lean Mechanization

Definition 1: `Objects/Reactor/Basic: Reactor`

Definition 2: `Objects/Reaction: Reaction`

Definition 3: `Objects/Change: Change.Normal`

Definition 4: not required in the mechanization

Definition 5: `Objects/Reactor/Basic: Reactor.StrictMember`

Definition 6: `Objects/Reactor/Hierarchical:`
`Reactor.Hierarchical`

Definition 7: `Objects/Reactor/Hierarchical:`
`Reactor.Hierarchical.obj?`

Definition 8: `Objects/Reactor/Proper: Reactor.Proper`

Definition 9: `Execution/Dependency: Dependency`

Definition 10: `Execution/State: Execution.State`

Definition 11: `Execution/Basic: Execution`

Definition 12: `Execution/State: Execution.State.Allows`

Definition 13: `Execution/State: Execution.State.Triggers`

Definition 14: `Execution/State: Execution.State.NextTag`

Definition 15: `Execution/Reactor: Reactor.Refresh`

Definition 16: `Execution/Theorems/Progress: Execution.Progress`

Definition 17: `Execution/State: Execution.State.Terminal`

Definition 18: `Execution/Dependency: Dependency`

Theorem 1:   `Execution/Theorems/Progress:`
`Execution.Progress.iff_deps_acyclic`

Theorem 2:   `Execution/Theorems/Execution:`
`Execution.deterministic`

Lemma 1:   `Execution/Theorems/Grouped/Instantaneous:`
`Execution.Instantaneous.Step.TC.deterministic`

Lemma 2:   `Execution/Theorems/Grouped/Instantaneous:`
`Execution.Instantaneous.Step.prepend_indep`

References

1. Abramsky, S., McCusker, G.: Game semantics. In: Berger, U., Schwichtenberg, H. (eds.) Computational Logic. NATO ASI Series, vol. 165, pp. 1–55. Springer, Heidelberg (1999). https://doi.org/10.1007/978-3-642-58622-4_1
2. Alur, R., et al.: The algorithmic analysis of hybrid systems. Theoret. Comput. Sci. **138**(1), 3–34 (1995)
3. Alur, R., Dill, D.L.: A theory of timed automata. Theoret. Comput. Sci. **126**(2), 183–235 (1994)
4. Baheti, R., Gill, H.: Cyber-physical systems. Impact Control Technol. **12**(1), 161–166 (2011)
5. Bai, Y.: Desynchronization: from macro-step to micro-step. In: 2018 16th ACM/IEEE International Conference on Formal Methods and Models for System Design (MEMOCODE), pp. 1–10. IEEE (2018)
6. Benveniste, A., Le Guernic, P.: A denotational theory of synchronous communicating systems (1987)
7. Benveniste, A., Le Guernic, P., Jacquemot, C.: Synchronous programming with events and relations: the signal language and its semantics. Sci. Comput. Program. **16**(2), 103–149 (1991)
8. Bergerand, J.L.: LUSTRE: un langage déclaratif pour le temps réel. Ph.D. thesis, Institut National Polytechnique de Grenoble-INPG (1986)
9. Bergstra, J.A., Ponse, A., Smolka, S.A.: Handbook of Process Algebra. Elsevier, New York (2001)
10. Berry, G., Cosserat, L.: The esterel programming language and its mathematical semantics. INRIA Res. Rep (327) (1984)
11. Borgida, A., Mylopoulos, J., Reiter, R.: On the frame problem in procedure specifications. IEEE Trans. Software Eng. **21**(10), 785–798 (1995). https://doi.org/10.1109/32.469460
12. Bourke, T., Brun, L., Dagand, P.É., Leroy, X., Pouzet, M., Rieg, L.: A formally verified compiler for lustre. In: Proceedings of the 38th ACM SIGPLAN Conference on Programming Language Design and Implementation, pp. 586–601 (2017)
13. Carneiro, M.: The type theory of lean (2019)
14. Cataldo, A., Lee, E., Liu, X., Matsikoudis, E., Zheng, H.: A constructive fixed-point theorem and the feedback semantics of timed systems. In: 2006 8th International Workshop on Discrete Event Systems, pp. 27–32. IEEE (2006)
15. Clinger, W.D.: Foundations of actor semantics. AITR-633 (1981)
16. Coquand, T., Huet, G.: The calculus of constructions. Inf. Comput. **76**(2-3) (1988)
17. Coquand, T., Paulin, C.: Inductively defined types. In: Martin-Löf, P., Mints, G. (eds.) COLOG 1988. LNCS, vol. 417, pp. 50–66. Springer, Heidelberg (1990). https://doi.org/10.1007/3-540-52335-9_47
18. Cremona, F., Lohstroh, M., Broman, D., Lee, E.A., Masin, M., Tripakis, S.: Hybrid co-simulation: it's about time. Softw. Syst. Model. **18**, 1655–1679 (2019)
19. Edwards, S.A.: On determinism. Principles of Modeling: Essays Dedicated to Edward A. Lee on the Occasion of His 60th Birthday, pp. 240–253 (2018)
20. Edwards, S.A., Hui, J.: The sparse synchronous model. In: 2020 Forum for Specification and Design Languages (FDL), pp. 1–8. IEEE (2020)
21. Ernst, R., Kuntz, S., Quinton, S., Simons, M.: The logical execution time paradigm: New perspectives for multicore systems (dagstuhl seminar 18092). In: Dagstuhl Reports, vol. 8. Schloss Dagstuhl-Leibniz-Zentrum fuer Informatik (2018)

22. Henzinger, T.A.: The theory of hybrid automata. In: Proceedings 11th Annual IEEE Symposium on Logic in Computer Science, pp. 278–292. IEEE (1996)
23. Hrbacek, K., Jech, T.: Introduction to Set Theory. Revised and Expanded. CRC Press, New York (2017)
24. Jagannathan, R.: Dataflow models. In: Parallel and Distributed Computing Handbook, pp. 223–238 (1995)
25. Kahn, G.: The semantics of a simple language for parallel programming. In: IFIP Congress (1974). https://api.semanticscholar.org/CorpusID:18030506
26. Kammar, O., Lindley, S., Oury, N.: Handlers in action. ACM SIGPLAN Not. **48**(9), 145–158 (2013)
27. Kirsch, C.M., Sokolova, A.: The logical execution time paradigm. In: Advances in Real-Time Systems, pp. 103–120 (2012)
28. Lamport, L.: How to write a 21st century proof. J. Fixed Point Theory Appl. **11**(1), 43–63 (2012). https://doi.org/10.1007/s11784-012-0071-6. http://link.springer.com/10.1007/s11784-012-0071-6
29. Lee, E., Messerschmitt, D.: Synchronous data flow. Proc. IEEE **75**(9), 1235–1245 (1987). https://doi.org/10.1109/PROC.1987.13876
30. Lee, E.A.: The past, present and future of cyber-physical systems: a focus on models. Sensors **15**(3), 4837–4869 (2015)
31. Lee, E.A.: Determinism. ACM Trans. Embed. Comput. Syst. (TECS) **20**(5), 1–34 (2021)
32. Lee, E.A., Lohstroh, M.: Time for all programs, not just real-time programs. In: Margaria, T., Steffen, B. (eds.) ISoLA 2021. LNCS, vol. 13036, pp. 213–232. Springer, Cham (2021). https://doi.org/10.1007/978-3-030-89159-6_15
33. Lee, E.A., Lohstroh, M.: Generalizing logical execution time. In: Raskin, J.F., Chatterjee, K., Doyen, L., Majumdar, R. (eds.) Principles of Systems Design. LNCS, vol. 13660, pp. 160–181. Springer, Cham (2023). https://doi.org/10.1007/978-3-031-22337-2_8
34. Lee, E.A., Zheng, H.: Operational semantics of hybrid systems. In: Morari, M., Thiele, L. (eds.) HSCC 2005. LNCS, vol. 3414, pp. 25–53. Springer, Heidelberg (2005). https://doi.org/10.1007/978-3-540-31954-2_2
35. Lohstroh, M.: Reactors: A Deterministic Model of Concurrent Computation for Reactive Systems (2020). https://doi.org/10.13140/RG.2.2.30520.78083. https://www.researchgate.net/publication/348155409
36. Lohstroh, M., et al.: Reactors: A Deterministic Model for Composable Reactive Systems (2020)
37. Lohstroh, M., Menard, C., Bateni, S., Lee, E.A.: Toward a lingua franca for deterministic concurrent systems. ACM Trans. Embed. Comput. Syst. (TECS) **20**(4), 1–27 (2021)
38. Lohstroh, M., et al.: Actors revisited for time-critical systems. In: Proceedings of the 56th Annual Design Automation Conference 2019, pp. 1–4 (2019)
39. Maler, O., Manna, Z., Pnueli, A.: Prom timed to hybrid systems. In: de Bakker, J.W., Huizing, C., de Roever, W.P., Rozenberg, G. (eds.) REX 1991. LNCS, vol. 600, pp. 447–484. Springer, Heidelberg (1992). https://doi.org/10.1007/BFb0032003
40. Menard, C., et al.: High-performance deterministic concurrency using lingua franca. arXiv preprint arXiv:2301.02444 (2023)
41. Moura, L., Ullrich, S.: The lean 4 theorem prover and programming language. In: Platzer, A., Sutcliffe, G. (eds.) CADE 2021. LNCS (LNAI), vol. 12699, pp. 625–635. Springer, Cham (2021). https://doi.org/10.1007/978-3-030-79876-5_37

42. Paulin-Mohring, C.: Introduction to the calculus of inductive constructions (2015)
43. Paulson, L.C.: Constructing recursion operators in intuitionistic type theory. J. Symb. Comput. **2**(4), 325–355 (1986)
44. Peterson, J.L.: Petri nets. ACM Comput. Surv. (CSUR) **9**(3), 223–252 (1977)
45. Pierce, B.C.: Types and Programming Languages. MIT Press, Cambridge (2002)
46. Pierce, B.C., et al.: Software foundations (2010). http://www.cis.upenn.edu/bcpierce/sf/current/index.html
47. Pilaud, D., Halbwachs, N., Plaice, J.: LUSTRE: a declarative language for programming synchronous systems. In: Proceedings of the 14th Annual ACM Symposium on Principles of Programming Languages (14th POPL 1987), vol. 178, p. 188. ACM, New York. Citeseer (1987)
48. Plotkin, G., Power, J.: Adequacy for algebraic effects. In: Honsell, F., Miculan, M. (eds.) FoSSaCS 2001. LNCS, vol. 2030, pp. 1–24. Springer, Heidelberg (2001). https://doi.org/10.1007/3-540-45315-6_1
49. Plotkin, G.D.: A structural approach to operational semantics. Aarhus university (1981)
50. Potop-Butucaru, D., De Simone, R., Talpin, J.P.: The synchronous hypothesis and synchronous languages. In: The Embedded Systems Handbook, pp. 1–21 (2005)
51. Ptolemaeus, C.: System Design, Modeling, and Simulation: Using Ptolemy II, vol. 1. Ptolemy.org, Berkeley (2014)
52. Ramadge, P., Wonham, W.: The control of discrete event systems. Proc. IEEE **77**(1), 81–98 (1989). https://doi.org/10.1109/5.21072
53. Scott, D.S.: Domains for denotational semantics. In: Nielsen, M., Schmidt, E.M. (eds.) ICALP 1982. LNCS, vol. 140, pp. 577–610. Springer, Heidelberg (1982). https://doi.org/10.1007/BFb0012801
54. Sozeau, M., Oury, N.: First-class type classes. In: Mohamed, O.A., Muñoz, C., Tahar, S. (eds.) TPHOLs 2008. LNCS, vol. 5170, pp. 278–293. Springer, Heidelberg (2008). https://doi.org/10.1007/978-3-540-71067-7_23
55. Tabuada, P.: Verification and Control of Hybrid Systems: A Symbolic Approach. Springer, New York (2009). https://doi.org/10.1007/978-1-4419-0224-5
56. Wadler, P.: Propositions as types. Commun. ACM **58**(12), 75–84 (2015)
57. Wadler, P.: Programming language foundations in Agda. In: Massoni, T., Mousavi, M.R. (eds.) SBMF 2018. LNCS, vol. 11254, pp. 56–73. Springer, Cham (2018). https://doi.org/10.1007/978-3-030-03044-5_5

Author Index

A. Reynolds and S. Tasiran (Eds.): VSTTE 2023, LNCS 14095, p. 109, 2024.
https://doi.org/10.1007/978-3-031-66064-1